THE P

THE PRESTIGE

screenplay by
Jonathan Nolan
and
Christopher Nolan

based on the novel by
Christopher Priest

faber and faber

First published in 2006
by Faber and Faber Limited
The Bindery, 51 Hatton Garden
London EC1N 8HN
Published in the United States by Faber and Faber Inc.
an affiliate of Farrar, Straus and Giroux LLC, New York

Typeset by Country Setting, Kingsdown, Kent CT14 8ES
Printed and bound by CPI Group (UK) Ltd, CR0 4YY

The right of Jonathan Nolan and Christopher Nolan to be identified
as authors of this work has been asserted in accordance with
Section 77 of the Copyright, Designs and Patents Act 1988

A CIP record for this book
is available from the British Library

ISBN 978-0-571-23582-7

Printed and bound in the UK on FSC® certified paper in line with our continuing
commitment to ethical business practices, sustainability and the environment.
For further information see faber.co.uk/environmental-policy

CONTENTS

INTRODUCTION

I'm probably not the best person to ask about how the script came together. I sat down to describe the process the other day and I had to keep correcting myself.

The work was difficult. I guess I can agree on at least that much. At times it felt like it was the first script I'd ever written, and I suppose, in a way, it was. Certainly the first book I'd ever adapted. Or, no, I guess not, although it certainly felt like it at times. But it wasn't easy. At first, nothing I did seemed to work. I wrote draft after draft, but I just couldn't make myself happy. I guess I'm my own harshest critic.

I first read Christopher Priest's novel in the fall of 2000, and then retold it to myself over a long walk near Highgate Cemetery, which would become the setting for one of Borden and Angier's encounters. I asked myself if it was the kind of story I was interested in. It was.

The first draft was a challenge. I gave myself strict instructions on how to proceed, but the novel contained so many ideas, so many interesting corners to get lost in. I tried to hold on to the modern-day storyline, at first easing it back a generation and setting it in post-war England. But early on I realised that to fit the novel into a projector would require concentrating on Borden and Angier. It would be their story, and theirs alone.

The first step of adapting a brilliant book is heresy – you have to throw it all out, then watch as, piece by piece, it creeps its way back in, with a smile, as if to say, 'I told you so.' The biggest challenge was the structure. The novel uses a deceptively simple narrative – one man tells the story; the next retells it from his own perspective. Of course, long after it's too late we realise we've been fooled – the structure is a fractal, folded down to resemble something simple. The truth has been hiding in plain sight. To achieve the same effect without using a present-day narrator as referee, the first draft used the three acts of the magic trick as a template. The final structure restored one of the key devices of the novel – the journals – allowing the protagonists to taunt each other from across the Atlantic and beyond the grave: Borden, in prison, waiting to hang, reading about Angier, in Colorado, waiting for Tesla to build his machine and, in turn, reading Borden's account of their early years.

Novelists must be somewhat appalled that, for the purposes of cinema, most of the nuance of their work is either blatantly ignored or hammered flat and pressed into the service of a story that can fit onto seven reels. So the séance – and the fascinating history of magicians taking up arms on either side of the question of where the stage ends – was replaced with a set-up that is bloodier and allows our protagonists a moment of friendship before the fun begins. The Alfred Borden of the novel will be shocked to discover that he's going to hang for the murder of his arch rival, although after discovering that the condemned prisoners' yard at Newgate was called the Birdcage Walk, how could I resist? Both Angier and Borden will be horrified to discover that their wives have been sacrificed on the altar of high drama. I tried to talk myself into sparing Sarah Borden, but my protests fell on deaf ears.

The women, in fact, provided the key to revising the script. In early drafts I abused them as heartlessly as Borden and Angier had ever done. I sent them off on errands, used them to nudge the story along, forced them to ferry messages back and forth between the protagonists. In subsequent drafts I concentrated on giving them back a little of the dignity and depth they had enjoyed in the novel. The final draft was, if I do say so myself, a dramatic improvement over my earlier efforts.

Both the book and the film ask you to invest equally in the two main characters. Due, however, to a quirk of western civilisation, we're only allowed one hero per story. So you'll have to decide, at some point, who you're rooting for. I went back and forth. In fact, I'm still not sure I really know who I side with. In earlier drafts Virgil, the magician who, for his finale, feeds birds into a collapsing cage, asks Borden to build him a cage big enough to 'vanish' a dog. Borden is, of course, disgusted, but at first the script functioned in the same way – the plot was a giant machine that collapsed on the two men, crushing them both. The final shot was the gaping mouth of an abandoned theatre into which Angier and Borden had disappeared. I argued with myself over it; one part of me wanted the end to be final, total; and the other part wanted a little light to escape. In the novel Christopher Priest allows one of the men to live on, albeit in a diminished capacity. In the end I followed suit, although, naturally, it wasn't the same magician who came back out of the box.

From the beginning, the film was conceived as a magic trick itself, and, in that sense, it's as if Priest entrusted us with the method to put on another version of his dazzling act. I go back and forth as to whether the finished script did justice to the wild and dark book that it's based on. I tell myself I did the best I could.

Jonathan and Christopher Nolan

The Prestige

The Prestige

Fade in:

Top hats. Clustered in a small glade. As we super titles, a black cat slinks its way through them. As titles end:

> BORDEN
> (*voice-over*)
> Are you watching closely?

A second black cat races into frame, hissing, spitting, chasing the first cat into the woods beyond and we –

Cut to:

INT. CLUTTERED WORKSHOP – DAY

Moving along a row of canaries in cages.

> CUTTER
> (*voice-over*)
> Every magic trick consists of three parts, or *acts* . . .

Stop at a cage. Weathered hands envelop the canary. Hands and voice belong to a man in his sixties – Cutter.

> CUTTER
> (*voice-over*)
> The first part is called the Pledge . . .

A Little Girl perches on a chest in the workshop, watching.

> The magician shows you something ordinary –

Cutter moves to a small ornate cage resting on a prop table.

> A deck of cards, or a bird . . .

INT. SCALA THEATRE, LONDON – NIGHT

A packed house. Many hands raised. Move in on a Bearded Man, his gloved hand tentatively rising into the air.

(*voice-over*)

. . . or a man.

A Glamorous Assistant beckons Bearded Man from the aisle. He shuffles along his row towards her. Embarrassed.

He shows you this object, and pledges to you its utter normality . . .

Bearded Man and four other Volunteers follow the Assistant down towards the stage . . .

On which stands the magician, leaning on his cane, smiling. This is Robert Angier, thirty-five, an American. Looming over him is a large and complex electrical machine.

Perhaps he asks you to inspect it . . .

Bearded Man, fascinated, and the other Volunteers look over the vast machine. As Angier gestures theatrically at the various features of the metal and glass apparatus –

. . . to see that it is indeed real . . .

As the Assistant leads the Volunteers off the stage, Bearded Man slips through the gap at the side of the curtains –

. . . unaltered . . .

INT. SCALA THEATRE, BACKSTAGE – CONTINUOUS

– looks around, disoriented, then darts for some stairs leading below stage where he runs into a burly Stagehand.

CUTTER
(*voice-over*)

. . . normal.

STAGEHAND
Where d'you think you're going?!

CUTTER
(*voice-over*)
But, of course, it probably isn't . . .

4

Bearded Man pulls off his beard and wig, revealing the face of Alfred Borden, mid-thirties.

BEARDED MAN
I'm part of the act, you fool!

The Stagehand raises his eyebrows and steps aside. Borden races down below the stage. Cutter approaches the Stagehand.

CUTTER
Who was that?

INT. SCALA THEATRE, ONSTAGE – CONTINUOUS

As the machine groans to life, sparking and crackling, Angier gazes at it, forgetting his audience. Entranced. Possessed.

INT. BENEATH THE STAGE – CONTINUOUS

Borden fumbles through the darkened area, lit by flashes and sparks through gaps in the boards of the stage above. He gasps as a flash illuminates a Stagehand with solid white eyes sitting nearby. Borden waves a hand in front of the Stagehand's face. He is blind. Borden moves on.

INT. WORKSHOP – DAY

Cutter gently places the canary into the ornate cage.

CUTTER
(*voice-over*)
The second act is called the Turn . . .

INT. SCALA THEATRE, ONSTAGE – NIGHT

Angier, facing the audience, steps into the machine.

CUTTER
(*voice-over*)
The magician takes the ordinary something . . .

5

INT. BENEATH THE STAGE – CONTINUOUS

Borden lights a match. In front of him is a large glass tank filled with water, its lid propped open. Borden frowns.

> CUTTER
> (*voice-over*)
> . . . and makes it do something extraordinary.

INT. WORKSHOP – DAY

Cutter places a silk shawl over the cage. Then slams his hands down on the shawl, which flattens. The Little Girl flinches. Then stares, fascinated.

> CUTTER
> (*voice-over*)
> Now you're looking for the secret.

INT. SCALA THEATRE, ONSTAGE – NIGHT

Bolts of electricity draw inwards, wrapping Angier in a ball of lightning which cracks.

> CUTTER
> (*voice-over*)
> But you won't find it . . .

INT. BENEATH THE STAGE – CONTINUOUS

The room fills with light as a trap-door snaps open and a body drops into the tank.

> CUTTER
> Because, of course, you're not really looking . . .

The lid of the tank and trap-door above snap shut, leaving the tank, and Borden, in complete darkness.

. . . you don't *really* want to know.

INT. WORKSHOP – DAY

Cutter whips the shawl from the table. Cage and bird have disappeared.

> CUTTER
> (*voice-over*)
> . . . You want to be fooled.

The Little Girl stares, expectant.

> But you wouldn't clap yet. Because making something
> disappear isn't enough . . . you have to bring it back.

INT. SCALA THEATRE, ONSTAGE – CONTINUOUS

*The machine sputters to a stop. Angier is gone. The audience sits,
waiting.*

> CUTTER
> (*voice-over*)
> That's why every magic trick has a third act. The hardest
> part . . .

INT. WORKSHOP – DAY

Cutter forms a fist. Drapes the shawl over it.

> CUTTER
> (*voice-over*)
> . . . the part we call . . .

*Cutter whips the shawl away to reveal – the canary. The Little Girl
claps.*

INT. BENEATH THE STAGE – NIGHT

Borden lights another match. Stares in horror.

> CUTTER
> (*voice-over*)
> . . . the Prestige.

Inside the tank, Angier is drowning. His rolling eyes fixed on Borden, he pounds desperately on the thick glass, screaming bubbles . . . The screen fades to black.

PROSECUTOR
(*voice-over*)

The Prestige . . .?

INT. COURTROOM – DAY

The Prosecutor turns to face the witness in the box: Cutter.

PROSECUTOR
And did Robert Angier, the Great Danton, your employer, get to that final part of his trick that night?

CUTTER
No, sir. Something went wrong.

PROSECUTOR
What went wrong?

CUTTER
I saw someone head below stage . . . I followed . . . and I found Borden –

Cutter points at the dock: Borden is there, chained to the floor. Flanked by guards. Cutter points.

– watching Mr Angier drown in a tank.

PROSECUTOR
Would you describe your occupation to the jury please, Mr Cutter?

CUTTER
I'm an *ingénieur*. I design illusions and construct the apparatus necessary for performing them.

PROSECUTOR
And for how long had you been Mr Angier's '*ingénieur*'?

CUTTER
Eight years. I was privy to the secrets of his entire act.

PROSECUTOR

So, Mr Cutter, was this water-filled tank beneath the stage part of Mr Angier's illusion – the illusion billed as 'The *Real* Transported Man'?

CUTTER

No, sir. The tank had been used for the first trick, then taken offstage. Borden must have put it under the trap-door after the interval.

Cutter looks across at Borden, who is absently tapping his hand against the rail – it is mutilated, missing two and a half fingers. The Defender stands.

DEFENDER

How large was this tank?

CUTTER

The sort of tank used for underwater escapes – four or five hundred gallons.

DEFENDER

How do you think Mr Borden was able to move the tank under the trap-door without anyone noticing?

CUTTER

Ask him – he's the magician.

Titters from the gallery. The Defender turns to the Judge.

DEFENDER
(*impatient*)

I ask again that this man explain the mechanics of Mr Angier's illusion.

CUTTER
(*angry*)

'The Real Transported Man' is the most sought-after illusion in the business – I have the right to sell it on – if I reveal the method here the trick will be worthless –

DEFENDER

With respect, Mr Cutter, we are talking about a capital offence – your financial gain cannot possibly –

CUTTER

I had a sacred trust with Robert Angier – it's my duty to
see that his secret be passed on to someone who'll respect
his memory, not plastered over the front page.

DEFENDER

How, then, can we know that the tank wasn't simply some
part of the trick that went wrong?

The Judge considers this. He looks at Cutter. Sympathetic.

JUDGE

Mr Cutter, I see your predicament, but Alfred Borden's life
hangs in the balance.

Cutter looks down. Quiet.

If you were prepared to disclose the details to me in private,
I might be able to judge their relevance to the case. (*Addresses
lawyers.*) Might this be an acceptable compromise?

Amid murmurs of assent, the Judge adjourns the proceedings.

*As the Guards begin the complex ritual of unlocking Borden's chains
from the floor, Borden looks across the courtroom.*

*The Little Girl from the opening stands in the gallery, looking back at
him. Borden gives her a little wave. She waves back, then is guided
out by a man wearing gloves and bowler hat – this is Fallon. He nods
at Borden.*

EXT. PRISON YARD, NEWGATE PRISON – DAY

*Heavy doors open to reveal Owens, fifties, a lawyer. The Captain of
the Guard leads him into the courtyard.*

CAPTAIN

I'm going to have to ask you to turn out your pockets.

*Owens raises his eyebrows as he hands over his pocket watch and
wallet for examination.*

Not my idea, sir. The Warden saw his show in Manchester
last year where he vanished into thin air – he's convinced
he'll try an escape.

The Captain hands them back as they walk across the courtyard and climb stairs to a walkway.

Across the courtyard a door opens and Borden emerges, trussed absurdly in chains held by two Warders. The other inmates begin cattle-calling and whistling as Borden is paraded up to a metal fence that crosses the walkway.

> I told him the only way Borden's going to disappear is if I leave him out here with the other inmates.

At the fence, the Warders lock the ends of their chains to a thick eye-hook set into the walkway.

> (*To Warders.*) Check the locks. Twice.

They check the locks. Then retreat to allow privacy. The Captain marches away. Borden looks at Owens. Bored.

OWENS
My name is Owens – I'm a solicitor.

Borden says nothing.

> I represent Lord Caldlow, an accomplished amateur magician and historian of magic –

BORDEN
How much?

OWENS
Lord Caldlow is interested in –

BORDEN
(*cold*)
How much for my tricks?

OWENS
Five thousand pounds.

BORDEN
Talk to Fallon, my *ingénieur* – the money's for him.

OWENS
I did. He offered to sell all of your tricks . . . except the most valuable one – 'The Transported Man'.

BORDEN

I'd never forgive myself for selling my greatest trick.

Borden signals the Warders to come and unlock him.

OWENS

Even for your daughter?

Borden looks up. Owens moves closer, quietly assertive.

If the newspapers are right, and you're for the drop, your daughter's going to need looking after –

BORDEN

Fallon can take care of –

OWENS

Bernard Fallon? A man with a past even more obscure than your own? The courts have already motioned to have the girl removed from his 'care'. No, the girl is to be an orphan. (*Looks at Borden.*) I believe you're no stranger to the inside of the workhouse . . .

Owens looks around the prison yard. Shrugs.

It's better than this.

Borden looks at Owens, hard. The Warders unlock Borden.

I'm offering you a way to wrap up your affairs with dignity, and I'm offering your daughter a future. As Lord Caldlow's ward she will want for nothing. Ever. (*Hands him a card.*) Think it over.

Borden absently vanishes the card as a reflex.

Lord Caldlow wanted you to have this – (*Produces a leather-bound journal.*) As a show of good faith. He thought it might be of interest.

A Sullen Warder takes the journal, flicks through it.

Robert Angier's diary . . . it includes the time he spent in Colorado learning your trick . . .

Sullen hands the journal to Borden. Borden takes it.

BORDEN

Angier never learned my trick.

OWENS

Really? When he returned from Colorado he mounted a version of 'The Transported Man' that the papers said was better, even . . . (*with relish*) than your original.

BORDEN
(*acid*)

If you want Angier's secret you can dig him up and ask him for yourself.

Borden turns, dragging the Warders with him.

OWENS

I want *your* secret, Mr Borden . . . (*Louder.*) Consider your daughter!

INT. CELL, NEWGATE PRISON – DAY

Borden, on the bed, opens Angier's journal. Starts to read . . .

ANGIER
(*voice-over*)

A cipher. An enigma . . .

INT. TRAIN, MOUNTAINS – DUSK

Angier opens his leather-bound journal. Starts to write.

ANGIER
(*voice-over*)

. . . Borden's cipher is simple – unravelled by a single word.

Angier reaches for a cardboard-bound notebook, opening it to reveal pages of letters in meaningless combinations. Gibberish with diagrams.

Now it takes only patience. And a passion to know his mind.

Angier looks up at his own reflection in the train window.

EXT. TRAIN STATION – DUSK

No platform, no office, no sign. Just an electric streetlight which, as Angier watches, flickers on. Angier, leaning heavily on his cane, limps over to the light and stares up at it as if he's never seen one before.

VOICE
(*out of shot*)
Mr Angier? Welcome to Colorado Springs.

Angier looks back and smiles. A driver is looking down expectantly from atop a stagecoach. Angier hands his cane up to the driver and, with some difficulty, hitches his way up to the roof of the rig. As he does, the town of Colorado Springs rises into view, a few hundred yards down the road, lit brightly with electric streetlights.

ANGIER
(*disbelief*)
The whole town has electricity?

The driver nods and whips the horses into action.

EXT. ROAD, PIKE'S PEAK – EVENING

The stagecoach flies along, inches from a precipitous drop.

It rounds a corner and pulls to a halt in front of the Cliff House inn, equal parts log cabin and crystal palace.

INT. CLIFF HOUSE INN – CONTINUOUS

The lobby is cavernous and immaculate. The entire staff of the hotel – Bellboys, Maids, Cooks and Gardeners – are lined up along the sides like a regiment of soldiers.

Angier reaches the reception desk and the smiling Manager.

ANGIER
Quite a reception.

MANAGER
You're our first guest of the season, Mr Angier. (*Opens guest book.*) Your telegram didn't indicate how long you would be staying with us.

ANGIER

As long as it takes. (*Signs book.*) I'll need a coach tomorrow
to take me up the mountain.

MANAGER

The peak is closed, sir. For scientific experimentation.

ANGIER
(*smiles*)

That's why I'm here.

EXT. ROAD, PIKE'S PEAK – MORNING

*A stagecoach rumbles along a dirt track. The driver pulls on his reins
and the coach pulls to a stop.*

DRIVER

You have to walk the rest, I'm afraid, sir.

Angier nods. Lowers himself down to the roadway.

EXT. CLEARING, PIKE'S PEAK – MORNING

Angier comes through the trees to find a wire fence with a sign:

EXTREME DANGER – NO TRESPASSING

*Beyond the fence is a compound of three barns. Rising from the centre
barn is a two-hundred-foot steel tower capped with a giant steel ball.
Giant arcing bolts of electricity run down the tower from the ball. The
windows of the building radiate with blue explosions.*

*Angier steps forwards, entranced, and threads his fingers through the
fence.*

He is sent flying backwards – the fence has been electrified.

*The tower is shut off – a door opens and a stout little man, shotgun
under one arm, marches up to the fence. He uses a rubber pad to pry
open the fence and stands over Angier, who is curled on the ground,
growling in pain, trying to stand.*

SHOTGUN

I'm amazed at how many of you newspaper writers can't
read my sign.

Shotgun picks up Angier's cane and hands it to him.

> ANGIER
>
> Not the welcome I was expecting.

Shotgun recognises Angier, amazed.

> SHOTGUN
>
> I know you. You're the Great Danton. (*Helps Angier up.*) I saw your show in London – seven times. You guessed every object the audience had in their pockets. I'm Alley.

Angier leans on his cane and gently brushes off the dirt.

> ALLEY
>
> Sorry about the fence – people keep interfering with our work.

> ANGIER
>
> I've come to see Tesla.

> ALLEY
>
> Why?

> ANGIER
>
> He built a machine for a – for a colleague of mine. A long time ago. Can you get me a meeting with him? (*Off his look.*) I've come a very long way.

> ALLEY
>
> Impossible, I'm afraid.

> ANGIER
>
> I've brought a lot of money.

Beat.

> ALLEY
>
> I'm sorry, Mr Angier. I simply can't help you.

Alley pulls the fence closed.

> ANGIER
>
> I'll be staying at the hotel. Indefinitely.

Alley watches Angier walk away. He pulls something from his pocket.

What am I holding?

Angier doesn't look back.

ANGIER

Your watch.

Alley grins, opening his hand. He is holding a gold watch.

INT. HOTEL ROOM, COLORADO – DAY

Angier sits, the cardboard-bound notebook on the table in front of him. He makes notations in his own journal as he deciphers Borden's words.

ANGIER
(*voice-over*)
April 3rd, 1897 . . . a few days after he first met me . . .

Angier runs his finger along the first line, translating . . .

BORDEN
(*voice-over*)
We were two young men at the start of a great career . . .

INT. THEATRE – NIGHT

Borden sits in the audience. Younger – both hands intact.

BORDEN
(*voice-over*)
Two young men devoted to an illusion . . .

Two rows in front sits Angier. Similarly youthful.

Two young men who never intended to hurt anyone.

Onstage is a tank. Standing beside the tank is a beautiful young magician's assistant. Julia.

The magician, Milton, address the audience.

MILTON
Which of you brave souls is willing to bind this lovely young woman?

Milton gestures to Julia – the men in the crowd go wild – hands in the air, catcalls. Smiling radiantly, Julia selects two young men, who scramble up to the stage – Angier and Borden: younger, full of energy. Angier has no limp.

They spring onto stage beside Julia and take the ropes she offers them. Milton grabs a hook that descends from the flies on a chain.

Cutter is watching from the wings.

Are either of you two gentlemen sailors?

Both shake their heads as they start to bind Julia with the ropes, Borden wrapping the rope around her wrists, Angier the one around her ankles.

Well, I'm sure you can both tie a strong knot . . .

As Borden finishes his knot, he tests it, and it slips apart. Borden frowns, hastily re-tying it, covering.

Cutter notices.

Borden finishes, glancing at Julia, who gives a small sign of assent with her eyes. As Angier finishes tying her ankles he sneaks a light kiss on her ankle. She frowns at him and raises her arms. Milton hooks the rope onto the chain.

Milton gesticulates – in the wings, Cutter signals to a Stagehand, who starts hoisting Julia into the air.

Milton wheels the tank under Julia's bare feet. Cutter feels for the handle of an axe placed by his feet and pulls out a stopwatch.

Julia looks down at Angier. They smile at each other. Julia drops into the tank with a massive splash – Milton slams the lid shut, padlocks it and raises a curtain around the tank . . .

Cutter checks his stopwatch, grips the handle of the axe . . .

A grand gesture from Milton – the curtain around the tank drops – Julia is gone. Milton raises the curtain again, then, with another flourish, drops it to reveal Julia, beside the tank, one arm in the air, dripping wet, smiling.

The audience erupts in applause. Angier smiles proudly.

INT. DRESSING ROOMS – NIGHT

Angier, Borden and Julia sit around the cluttered room. Borden is in the middle of a passionate rant:

> BORDEN
>
> Milton's squandering their goodwill on a bunch of tired second-hand tricks –

> ANGIER
> *(amused)*
>
> Old favourites, please.

> BORDEN
>
> What about something fresh? He won't even try a bullet-catch –

> CUTTER
> *(out of shot)*
>
> Bullet-catch is suicide.

They turn. Cutter stands in the doorway, counting out money.

> All it takes is a smart-arse volunteer dropping a button down the barrel . . .

> BORDEN
> *(indicates himself and Angier)*
>
> Use plants –

> ANGIER
>
> He can't use plants for *every* trick.

> JULIA
>
> There'd be no seats left for the punters.

> BORDEN
>
> Fine – no bullet-catch. But a real magician tries to invent something new, something other magicians scratch their heads over –

> CUTTER
>
> Then sells it to them for a small fortune.

Cutter hands Angier some money.

I suppose you have such a trick, Mr Borden?

                    BORDEN
Actually, I do.

                    CUTTER
Care to sell it?

                    BORDEN
No one else could do my trick.

                    ANGIER
Any trick can be duplicated. Right, Mr Cutter?

Cutter looks at Borden, thoughtful. Shrugs.

                    CUTTER
If Borden here really *has* invented his masterpiece it might
well be something only he can do.

                    ANGIER
Why?

                    CUTTER
It might be something only he is prepared to do. (*Gestures
to the props.*) Milton's a skilled showman. But Borden's
right – he won't get his hands dirty. You want to see what
it takes to make real magic – go to the Tenley. There's a
Chinaman there who's got what it takes.

                    ANGIER
Chung Ling Soo.

                    BORDEN
Tickets are pricey.

                    CUTTER
I know a lad on the door. You two watch his show –
whoever tells me how he does his goldfish bowl trick gets
the prize.

                    ANGIER
Which is?

Cutter gives a sly smile.

CUTTER

Ten minutes onstage in front of my old friend, Mr
Ackerman.

Angier and Borden prick up at the name.

JULIA

Who's Ackerman?

BORDEN

The most powerful theatrical agent in London.

*Cutter holds out money to Borden, who reaches for it – Cutter grabs
his wrist. Serious.*

CUTTER

I saw you drop the knot again, Borden.

JULIA

I think I had my wrist turned –

CUTTER
(*ignoring Julia*)

Some nights you just can't get it, can you? If the knot slips
when Julia's on the hoist she'll break a leg.

BORDEN
(*defensive*)

It's the wrong knot. A Langford double would hold tighter.

CUTTER

The Langford double's not a wet knot – it's too dangerous.
The ropes could swell and she'd never slip it –

JULIA

I can slip a Langford underwater.

BORDEN

We'll practise during –

ANGIER
(*harsh*)

He said no.

Borden turns to glare at Angier. Challenging.

BORDEN

Know your knots better than me, do you? Want to take over?

Angier says nothing.

Didn't think so.

CUTTER
(*to Borden*)

No more mistakes.

Borden stares at Cutter. Leaves. Angier watches him go.

ANGIER

Where's he from?

CUTTER

Where are you from?

Angier nods. Fair enough.

He shuffles props for Virgil at the Hall.

ANGIER

Aren't you worried he'll steal your tricks?

CUTTER
(*shakes head*)

He doesn't deal in methods.

ANGIER

How do you know?

CUTTER
(*sly smile*)

Because I hired him to try and find out Virgil's orange trick.

ANGIER

I don't know if I trust him.

CUTTER

He's a natural magician. Of course you can't trust him.

JULIA

I think he's alright.

Angier turns to Julia. Smiles.

> ANGIER
>
> You think everyone's alright.

> JULIA
>
> Even you.

Julia kisses Angier. Cutter rises.

> CUTTER
>
> And Mr Angier . . . ?

Angier looks up.

> Learn your sightlines – if I can see you sneaking a peck on
> your wife's ankle from the wings, the blokes on each end of
> rows three and four can, too.

INT. STRAND THEATRE – DAY

*Borden watches from the wings. Onstage, a magician, Virgil, locks a
canary into a cage then covers the cage with a shawl.*

*Borden notices a beautiful Young Woman in the front row with a Little
Boy who is watching Virgil's act, spellbound.*

*Virgil slams the shawl down onto the table, as if nothing were beneath
it, then whips it away – bird and cage are gone.*

The Little Boy begins to wail and cry.

*Borden watches as the Young Woman tries to make him stop. Virgil
takes the flower from his lapel, covers it with the shawl, and snaps it
away – the flower has become the canary.*

*The audience bursts into enthusiastic applause, but the Little Boy is
still crying inconsolably. Virgil takes his bows and walks off, handing
Borden the canary as he passes backstage. As the audience leaves,
Borden climbs off the stage and holds the bird in front of the boy.*

> BORDEN
>
> Look – he's alright. He's fine.

BOY
(*sniffs*)
But where's his brother?

Borden is at a loss. He turns to the Young Woman.

BORDEN
Sharp lad, your son.

YOUNG WOMAN
(*laughs*)
My nephew.

Borden smiles back.

INT. VIRGIL'S DRESSING ROOM, STRAND THEATRE – MOMENTS
LATER

Borden gently strokes the bird's feathered head.

BORDEN
You're the lucky one today.

Borden walks to a wall of dozens of birdcages – each one with an identical canary. He puts the bird into its cage and returns to the cart of props. He taps on the top of the table – a panel pops open, revealing the flattened birdcage.

Borden inserts a rod into the birdcage and pries it apart. A trickle of blood emerges, dripping into a bucket below.

Borden slaps the cage –

– and the flattened carcass of the original bird slides out and splashes into the bucket.

EXT. STAGE DOOR, STRAND THEATRE – DAY

Borden exits. The young woman, Sarah, is there with her nephew.

BORDEN
(*to the Boy*)
Are you watching closely?

Borden reaches to the Boy's ear. Casually produces a coin. The Boy marvels as he takes the coin, then looks at Borden.

Look closer.

                    BOY
It's got two heads.

Sarah smiles. Borden crouches to address the Boy, grave.

                    BORDEN
Never. Show. Anyone.

The Boy looks at him, a little afraid.

They'll beg you and flatter you for the secret – but as soon as you give it up you'll be nothing to them. Understand? Nothing. The secret impresses no one – the trick you use it for is everything.

Borden looks into the Boy's staring eyes. Then smiles and pats him on the head. He stands. Sarah smiles at him.

Where do you two live?

                    SARAH
He lives with his mum.

                    BORDEN
And you?

INT. STAIRWELL – DAY

Sarah and Borden come up the stairs to her flat.

                    SARAH
Thank you for lunch, Mr Borden.

                    BORDEN
You're welcome. And it's Alfred.

They arrive outside her door. Sarah opens it.

I could use a cup of tea.

Sarah smiles at him.

SARAH

Scandalise the landlord? I think not.

She steps inside. Borden tests the lock of the open door.

BORDEN

Enough to keep me out?

SARAH

I think so. Will I see you again?

Borden shrugs and turns down the stairs. Sarah looks after him, about to change her mind. Hesitates.

INT. SARAH'S FLAT – CONTINUOUS

She closes the door and locks it, smiling. After a moment she pads through living area, draws back the curtain to her kitchen and shrieks:

Borden is there, smiling, holding the kettle.

BORDEN

Milk and sugar?

Sarah moves towards him, giggling.

INT. TENLEY THEATRE – NIGHT

Onstage, Chung Ling Soo, sixties, wearing a long silk robe, hobbles painfully to the centre of the stage. Clearly crippled. In the audience, Borden and Angier watch intently.

Soo lays a silk shawl on a bare table. He whips it up, revealing a bouquet of roses. Soo repeats the trick again and again, producing a different object each time.

Finally, with a drum roll, Soo whips the shawl aside to reveal a massive goldfish bowl, complete with goldfish.

To thunderous applause, Soo bows and hobbles off the stage. Angier, clapping, shakes his head, utterly baffled. He turns to Borden. Who has a small, knowing, smile.

26

EXT. RESTAURANT – NIGHT

Borden and Angier watch Soo being helped down from his carriage by Handlers who treat him with great gentleness.

> ANGIER
>
> You're wrong. It can't be.

> BORDEN
>
> It is. He carries the bowl between his knees for the entire performance.

> ANGIER
>
> But look at the man!

> BORDEN
> (*points*)
>
> This is the trick. This is why no one detects his method.

Soo hobbles into the restaurant, frail and fragile.

> Total devotion to his art . . . (*Looks at Angier.*) Utter self-sacrifice. It's the only way to escape *this*.

Borden slaps the bricks of the wall behind them.

INT. BEDSIT – NIGHT

Julia, in bed, watches Angier, sheet wrapped around him like a robe, hobbling. He pulls up the sheet – between his knees is a goldfish bowl.

> ANGIER
>
> I can barely lift this thing and it's not even filled with water. Or fish. He must be strong as an ox.

> JULIA
> (*incredulous*)
>
> He's been pretending to be a cripple for years?

> ANGIER
>
> Any time he's in public. Any time he goes out. It's *unthinkable*.

Angier puts the bowl down with a flourish. Climbs into bed.

Borden saw it at once. I couldn't fathom it – living your whole life pretending to be someone else.

                              JULIA

You're pretending to be someone else.

                              ANGIER

I don't think changing your name compares –

                              JULIA

Not just your name – who you are, where you're from . . .

                              ANGIER

I promised my family I wouldn't embarrass them with my theatrical endeavours.

Angier cuddles up to Julia.

                              JULIA

I came up with a name for you . . . 'The Great Danton'.

Angier frowns.

You don't like it? It's sophisticated.

                              ANGIER

It's French.

INT. SARAH'S FLAT – DAY

Sarah unlocks the door, but has to push against magical props stacked against it – the bedsit is filled with devices.

                              SARAH

Alfred?!

Sarah surveys the confusion – spots Borden across the flat, deep in conversation with another man. Borden spots her.

                              BORDEN

We have our first booking!

The other man turns – it is Fallon.

                              SARAH
                              (*cold*)

We haven't had the pleasure.

28

Fallon nods. Borden comes over, holding a duelling pistol.

BORDEN

Mr Fallon is my *ingénieur* –

SARAH

Where did you get all of –

BORDEN

Begged, borrowed and don't ask. Mr Fallon's an enterprising soul. (*Excited.*) It's a little theatre – well, more of a pub, really – but it's a start, and if Cutter makes good on his promise to bring Ackerman down to see it –

SARAH

I need to talk to you.

Fallon slips past Sarah with a nod to Borden. Exits. Sarah looks at Borden. Tense.

We can't afford to pay him –

BORDEN

We'll start making money once we have our audience –

SARAH

And until then? What I earn is barely enough for us.

BORDEN
(*shrugs*)

I'll give him half of my food.

Sarah looks meaningfully at Borden.

SARAH

You're already going to be sharing it with someone else.

Borden looks at her, confused. Then realises.

BORDEN

You're . . .?

SARAH

Having a baby.

Borden freezes. Then smiles, taking her in his arms. She flinches against the gun he is holding.

SARAH

What's this?

BORDEN

The trick to wake up Ackerman at the end of my act.

SARAH

Your great trick? The 'masterpiece that will make our fortunes'?

BORDEN

No. The world isn't ready for that one, yet.

Borden moves to the bureau and starts loading the gun. Pouring in shot, then wadding . . .

This is merely a run-of-the-mill daring and spectacular bullet-catch –

Borden drops the bullet into the barrel . . .

SARAH

I'm not letting you get shot.

Borden rams the bullet and charge down, then removes the ramrod and hands the pistol to Sarah.

BORDEN

It's perfectly safe. Shoot me.

Sarah looks at Borden then down at the pistol. She aims at Borden. Then aims off, at a mirror beside him.

Bang. Borden's hand snaps out to 'catch' the bullet. The mirror is intact.

Borden looks at Sarah, grave, as he reveals the bullet in his hand.

SARAH

Show me.

Borden shakes head.

Then you're not doing it. I can't raise a child on my own, Alfred.

Borden looks at her. Takes the bullet from her and places it on the bureau.

> BORDEN
> The bullet goes in the gun. Then comes the ramrod . . .

He takes the ramrod and pushes it down onto the bullet, which disappears.

> And *voilà* –

He points the ramrod at Sarah – she pulls the bullet out of its hollow tip.

> The bullet's not even in the gun when the charge is fired.

Sarah looks at the ramrod with disdain.

> SARAH
> Once you know it's so obvious.

Borden bristles slightly. Takes the bullet back.

> BORDEN
> Yes, well, people still get killed performing it.

> SARAH
> How?

> BORDEN
> Some smart-arse drops something down the barrel.

> SARAH
> Such as?

> BORDEN
> A penny, or a button. Or, of course, a bullet. (*Off worried look.*) But don't fret –

Borden embraces her, putting his hand on her belly.

> I'm not letting anything happen – I love you too much.

Sarah grabs his face, looking at his eyes, smiling.

> SARAH
> Say it again.

                    BORDEN

I love you.

                    SARAH
                (matter-of-fact)

Nope. Not today.

                    BORDEN

What?

                    SARAH
                (smiles)

Some days, it's not true. Today you don't mean it. Maybe
today you're more in love with magic than me. *(Off look.)*
It's alright. I like being able to tell the difference – it makes
the days it *is* true mean something.

Borden shakes his head, grinning.

INT. HOTEL ROOM, COLORADO – NIGHT

*Angier closes Borden's notebook. He looks across at a photograph of
Julia on the table. Reaches for his own diary.*

                    ANGIER
                (voice-over)

Borden writes as if no one but he understood the true
nature of magic . . .

INT. CELL, NEWGATE PRISON – DAY

Borden sits on his cot reading Angier's journal.

                    ANGIER
                (voice-over)

. . . but what does he know of self-sacrifice more than the
rest of us?

Borden looks up from Angier's journal.

                    BORDEN

Bloody fool.

Borden tosses the book across the cell.

INT. EVIDENCE ROOM, WAREHOUSE – DAY

A Policeman opens the door for the Judge and Cutter.

> POLICEMAN
> (*pointing*)
> It's all laid out down the end, your honour.

The Judge nods. The Policeman exits, locking them inside.

The Judge follows Cutter, approaching a collection of magical apparatus, including a massive crate. Cutter looks up at it with awe, touching the side where it says COLORADO SPRINGS.

> JUDGE
> What's in there?

Cutter opens it, revealing metal and glass machinery within.

> CUTTER
> Angier's machine.

> JUDGE
> You built this, Mr Cutter?

> CUTTER
> (*shakes head*)
> Oh no. This wasn't built by a magician . . . it was built by a wizard. (*Off look.*) A man who can actually do the things a magician pretends to.

Cutter closes the crate. The Judge turns to other props.

> Your honour, what will happen to these things when the trial is over?

The Judge is staring at a large glass tank.

> JUDGE
> They've been sold to a Lord Caldlow. An avid collector, apparently very interested in the case.

CUTTER

Don't let him take this.

The Judge looks over. Cutter is touching the crate.

JUDGE

Why ever not?

CUTTER

It's dangerous.

JUDGE

I'm sure beneath its bells and whistles it's got some simple and disappointing trick.

CUTTER

The most disappointing of all – it has no trick. It's real.

The Judge looks at Cutter. Smiles indulgently. Turns.

JUDGE

This is the tank Angier drowned in?

Cutter turns to look at the empty, smashed glass of the tank. Nods. Cutter indicates the top of the tank, where there is a padlock. Cutter pushes down on a panel of the lid.

CUTTER

This lets the performer's hands reach the trick padlock – a small section pops open.

JUDGE

A standard magical apparatus for escapes?

CUTTER

With one important difference . . .

Cutter grabs the padlock. Rattles it.

This isn't a trick lock . . . it's been switched out for a *real* one.

The Judge stares at the tank, appalled.

JUDGE

What a way to kill someone. Why in God's name go to such lengths?

CUTTER

These are magicians, your honour. Showmen. Men who live by dressing up plain and sometimes brutal truths to amaze. To shock.

JUDGE

Even without an audience?

Cutter stares at the tank.

Insert cut: Angier screaming bubbles.

CUTTER

There was an audience. (*Looks at Judge.*) See, the water tank had a particular significance for the two men . . .

INT. THEATRE – EVENING

Onstage, a similar tank filled with water.

CUTTER
(*voice-over*)

A particularly awful significance . . .

Julia stands next to the tank. Milton addresses the audience.

MILTON

Which of you brave souls is willing to bind this lovely young woman?

Milton gestures to Julia – the crowd goes wild. Julia makes a show of deciding. She picks Angier and Borden, who are made up to look different from the last performance. As they leap up onto the stage, Borden makes eye contact with Cutter in the wings – Cutter's is a warning glance.

As Angier ties Julia's ankles he can't resist tickling just under her toes – she kicks him in the chin.

Borden starts to wrap the rope around Julia's wrists in a particular fashion. Stops. Reconsiders. Julia nods at him, encouraging. Borden starts re-tying the knot.

Cutter watches. His hand checking for the axe handle.

Borden tests the rope – it is tight. Julia gives him the sign with her eyes – he steps back. Angier rises to his feet, grinning at Julia. As she raises her arms to the hook, she can't quite hide her smile back at him.

Milton gives the sign and Julia is hoisted into the air. Cutter slips his stopwatch out of his pocket as Milton moves the tank under Julia's bare feet.

Angier looks up at Julia. Proud. She stares out over the audience, preparing herself. Looks down at Angier, smiling . . .

Julia plunges into the tank – Milton slams the lid shut – Cutter checks his stopwatch, hand caressing the axe handle . . .

Milton raises the curtain around the tank, then circles it, working his 'magic'. Angier shifts a little. Time passing . . . Milton looks at Cutter – too much time . . .

Cutter grasps his axe and sprints at the tank – Milton rips the curtain down – Julia, one arm free, is convulsing . . .

Angier and Borden look on in horror as Cutter swings his axe into the glass – which cracks . . . Cutter swings again and again – the web of cracks growing, Julia's convulsions slowing, her eyes pleading with Angier's, until –

Crash – the glass gives way, flooding the stage – Cutter and Angier grasp at Julia – pull her onto the stage – Cutter elbows Angier out of the way to pound on Julia's chest – Borden watches, stunned, as Julia flops, lifeless, onto the boards. Cutter looks up at Angier, stricken.

Angier takes Julia in his arms, looking down at her staring eyes. He desperately brushes water from Julia's cheeks and forehead. Borden looks on, ashen.

INT. BATHROOM, LONDON – DAY

Angier has his head submerged in a sink full of water. He bursts free, gasping – collapses to the floor, sobbing.

INT. MAUSOLEUM – DAY

Julia is laid out. Mourners maintain a discreet distance as Angier stands over her. Cutter, at his shoulder, watches his distress.

CUTTER

I knew an old sailor. Told me about a time he got pulled
over the side tangled in the sheets . . . they dragged him
out, but it was five minutes before he coughed . . .

Angier looks up at Cutter. Hanging.

He said it was like . . . going home.

*Angier looks at Cutter. Comforted. Cutter spots something – Angier
follows his gaze to see Borden stepping forward.*

What are you doing, Borden?

BORDEN

I'm sorry for your loss, Angier.

Angier stares at Borden.

ANGIER

Which knot did you tie?

Borden shifts, glances down.

BORDEN

I keep asking myself that.

ANGIER
(*quiet*)

And?

BORDEN

And I'm sorry, but I just don't know.

ANGIER

Don't know?!

BORDEN

I'm sorry.

Borden backs away through the other mourners.

ANGIER

DON'T KNOW?!

Angier's voice echoes through the mausoleum.

INT. BATHROOM – DAY

Angier stands before the mirror, practising a movement with his hand. He performs the movement again and again, his eyes cold. He is practising concealing and producing a small lead shot.

EXT. PRINCE'S ARMS BAR AND THEATRE – NIGHT

A crude sign leaning against the wall:

> THURSDAYS
> 'THE PROFESSOR' PERFORMS
> FEATS OF MAGIC AND MYSTERY
> INCLUDING HIS RENOWNED
> DEATH-DEFYING BULLET-CATCH!

INT. PRINCE'S ARMS BAR AND THEATRE

Rough. Unwelcoming. Crowded. A small 'stage' at one end. Borden works his way through the Chinese rings. The crowd is jeering.

VOICE

Get out your gun, Professor!

Someone hurls a bottle at the stage – it narrowly misses. Borden glares out into the audience. Pulls out his gun.

BORDEN

A volunteer.

The crowd surges forward with eager volunteers. Fallon scans the crowd, passing over the too-eager and too-drunk before settling on a Moustached Man and bringing him up onstage.

Borden loads the pistol, hands it to Moustache and steps backwards, pulling his coat apart, challenging.

Are you man enough, sir?

MOUSTACHED MAN
(*quiet*)

Yes.

*Something in Moustache's tone makes Borden look closely – behind
the moustache . . . Angier. Quivering with tension.*

ANGIER

Which knot did you tie, Borden?

Borden looks at the trembling gun. Then at Angier. Spreads his hands.

BORDEN
(*sincere*)

I don't know.

Angier purses his lips, straining to pull the trigger.

Insert cut: Julia's face, screaming bubbles . . .

Angier's eyes are almost closed as he squeezes the trigger.

*Fallon hits Angier's wrist – the gun roars – Borden screams as his
right hand explodes.*

*Pandemonium. Fallon jumps to Borden's side, grabbing his bleeding
hand. The crowd is screaming, pushing for the door, or straining for
a closer look at Borden.*

*Angier, shocked, melts into the crowd. As Fallon tries to staunch the
bleeding, Borden's face is contorted in agony.*

BORDEN
(*voice-over*)

He came to demand an answer. And I told him the truth . . .
that I've fought with myself over that night . . . one half of
me swearing blind that I tied a simple slip knot . . . the
other half convinced that I tied the Langford double. I can
never know for sure –

INT. HOTEL ROOM, COLORADO – DAY

Angier looks up from Borden's journal, despairing.

ANGIER

How can he not know?!

Angier flings Borden's journal across the room.

                        BORDEN
                      (*voice-over*)
He must know what he did. He must.

INT. PRISON CELL – DAY

Borden smiles as he reads Angier's diary.

                        BORDEN
'How can he not know?!' (*Starts laughing.*) Because, Angier,
life is complicated, people are complicated, knots are
complicated –

                        PRISONER
                      (*out of shot*)
Shut it, Professor, or I'll shut it for you.

Borden quiets. Looking at the journal.

                        BORDEN
                      (*voice-over*)
How could I not know? How can you read my story and
not understand?

INT. COURTROOM – DAY

*Cutter sits in the crowded gallery. Borden, in the dock, scans the
crowd. Finally spots Fallon pushing to the front – he is alone. Borden
stares at him. Fallon shakes his head.*

*Borden is prompted to stand by two Guards as the Judge enters. The
Judge has a piece of black cloth draped over his wig.*

                        JUDGE
Alfred Borden, you have been found guilty of the murder of
Robert Angier. You will, in one month's time, be hanged by
the neck until dead. May the Lord have mercy on your
soul.

Borden barely reacts.

EXT. PRISON YARD, NEWGATE PRISON – DAY

Borden stands at the fence with Fallon.

> BORDEN
>
> They took her away?

Fallon nods.

> To the workhouse?

Another slow nod. Borden closes his eyes with despair. Then opens them and hands Fallon Owens' card.

> Tell him I've reconsidered. (*Off look.*) It's for the best.

INT. DINING ROOM, CLIFF HOUSE INN, COLORADO SPRINGS – DUSK

Angier stares down at the notebook, making notes in his own journal. Through large windows a thunderstorm batters Pike's Peak. Angier is the only guest in the massive dining room.

> VOICE
> (*out of shot*)
>
> Mind if I join you?

Angier looks around. Alley is standing by the table.

> ALLEY
>
> Tesla sends me down here during the storms. Perfect excuse to come share a drink with the Great Danton.

Alley sits, gesturing to a Waiter.

> Have you tried our bourbon yet, Mr Angier? It matches the scenery nicely. (*To Waiter.*) Two of 'em. (*To Angier.*) Beautiful, isn't it? I do miss New York, though.

> ANGIER
>
> Why are you here?

> ALLEY
>
> The lightning lives here. And not much else – our work is secret.

Alley glances down at the notebook and Angier's scribbles.

A cipher?

Angier nods as Alley lifts the cardboard notebook.

> ANGIER
> My profession also deals in secrets.

Alley looks at the gibberish on the pages of the notebook.

> It's a rotating transposition that shifts every day of the
> diary. Simple but time-consuming to translate once you
> have the five-letter keyword.

> ALLEY
> Which is?

Angier smiles as he reaches for the notebook.

> ANGIER
> We magicians have a circle of trust.

> ALLEY
> You have a circle of trust with someone whose diary you
> stole?

> ANGIER
> Maybe I bought it.

> ALLEY
> Magicians sell their secrets?

> ANGIER
> It's how we pay for our retirements and how great tricks
> outlive us.

Alley considers this. Taps the cover of the notebook.

> ALLEY
> You're hoping to find a great secret in there?

> ANGIER
> I've already found it. That's why I'm here.

*Angier reaches in his pocket and removes his own, leather-bound
journal. He tears a page from it and hands it to Alley, who unfolds it
and stares at it.*

Tesla built one for another magician.

ALLEY
Why would you want the same thing?

ANGIER
Call it a professional rivalry.

ALLEY
Tesla has built unusual machines for unusual people, but he would never talk about it.

ANGIER
I understand discretion. I just want the machine.

Alley looks at Angier. Thinking.

ALLEY
Finish your drink. You'll have a special appreciation for our work.

ANGIER
I thought it was a secret.

ALLEY
(*smiles*)
You're a magician. Who's going to believe you?

EXT. FIELDS, COLORADO SPRINGS – NIGHT

The storm has abated. Angier's cane sinks into the muddy ground as he follows Alley through the moonlit field.

There are large glass globes pushing out of the soil, as if planted, all around them. They stop in the middle of the field, looking down at the electric lights of the town.

ALLEY
We do our tests when the townspeople are asleep – Mr Tesla doesn't want to scare anyone.

Alley checks his watch by the moonlight.

Not long now.

As they watch, the lights of Colorado Springs disappear.

>Our equipment requires a great deal of current. Tesla electrified the whole town in exchange for using the generators when we need to.

The field around them explodes with dazzling light. Angier laughs out in surprise – the field is full of a thousand large lightbulbs, all glowing together. Alley bends down and picks up the nearest lightbulb – as he does, the light in it extinguishes. He tosses the bulb to Angier. Except for the size, it's a normal lightbulb.

>ANGIER

Where are the wires?

>ALLEY

Exactly.

Angier bends and gently pushes the lightbulb into a random spot in the wet soil. The lightbulb flickers on again.

>ANGIER

Where's the generator?

>ALLEY

You saw it last week.

>ANGIER

But that must be ten miles from here.

>ALLEY

Fifteen. And I have to ride all of them before I get to bed. (*Turns to leave.*) I'll send word for you in a few days, Mr Angier.

Angier bends to pick up his lightbulb. As he does, the light fades in all of them, and the lights in town come back on. Angier is alone.

INT. PUB – DAY

Angier sits at the bar. Staring. He raises his pint glass. Downs it, then stops, looking at the bottom – there is a playing card. He looks around. Cutter is sitting at a table with two fresh pints in front of him. Angier heads over.

ANGIER

Never thought I'd find an answer at the bottom of a pint glass.

CUTTER

Hasn't stopped you looking.

Angier sits.

(*out of shot*)

I heard about a booking. Nice little theatre. Good up-and-coming magician.

ANGIER

Who?

CUTTER

You.

ANGIER

You got me a booking? Why?

Cutter looks down into his beer.

CUTTER

Because I want to keep working . . . (*Looks up at Angier.*) And who's going to hire the *ingénieur* who killed Julia McCullough in front of a sellout crowd at the Orpheum?

Angier looks back at Cutter.

ANGIER

Someone who knows that it wasn't your fault. Someone who knows Alfred Borden and his repertoire of exotic knots.

CUTTER

Heard he had a spot of bad luck doing a bullet-catch south of the river.

Angier looks down at the liquid in his glass.

ANGIER

Dangerous trick, that one.

INT. WORKSHOP – DAY

Angier and Cutter inspect a large empty room.

CUTTER

We'll have to whitewash the windows to confound the more curious members of your audience . . . (*Looks around.*) But this should do.

ANGIER

We should see about an assistant.

CUTTER

I've made arrangements. Have you settled on a name?

ANGIER

Yes, I have. The Great Danton.

CUTTER

Hmm. Bit old-fashioned?

Angier smiles gently at Cutter.

ANGIER

No. It's sophisticated.

INT. SARAH'S FLAT – DAY

Sarah is frantically redressing Borden's injured hand. Blood has seeped through the bandages.

SARAH

I don't understand, Alfred. How can it be bleeding again?

She examines the wounds: two and a half fingers are missing. The injuries are black, but wet and fresh.

What have you been doing to it? It looks as bad as the day it happened. We need to get the doctor back –

BORDEN
(*snaps*)

We can't *afford* the doctor back!

A baby starts crying in the bedroom. Sarah glares at Borden.

46

SARAH

You've woken her.

BORDEN

I'm sorry. I just need this to heal so I can get back to work.

Sarah looks at Borden. Reluctantly:

SARAH

Alfred, you have to face things. What tricks could you perform with this kind of injury?

BORDEN

Some of the card pulls, prop tricks . . . (*Leans forward, excited.*) And the trick I've been telling you about. The trick they'll remember me for.

INT. ANGIER'S WORKSHOP – DAY

Angier is sitting at a worktable, pensive. He is moving one hand across the other, making a rose appear and disappear. The windows have been whitewashed and the room has filled with an array of magical apparatus: cabinets, costumes, props.

On the other side of the room Cutter watches as Olivia Wenscombe, twenties, equal parts grace and mischief, squeezes herself into a tall cabinet, looking past Cutter to Angier.

OLIVIA

What's so hard about this?

Cutter leans into the cabinet and pops up a trick panel in the floor, revealing a tiny chamber.

CUTTER

In here, Miss Wenscombe. No point meeting Mr Angier unless you fit.

Olivia shrugs and hands Cutter her hat, then her thick skirts, and folds herself into the bottom of the box.

Breathe as little as possible.

Cutter closes the lid over her and walks over to Angier.

47

Not much experience, but she knows how to present herself and a pretty assistant's the most effective form of misdirection.

Angier nods. There is a small sneeze from inside the cabinet.

(*Smiles.*) I suppose I should let her out.

INT. ANGIER'S WORKSHOP – DAY

Angier and Cutter, at the workbench, examine a birdcage. Cutter is wearing a strange leather harness over his shirt: it has large springs and small pulleys on the back.

ANGIER
The birdcage can't be our climax – everybody knows it.

CUTTER
Not like this, they don't.

ANGIER
And I don't want to kill doves.

CUTTER
(*snaps*)
Then stay off the stage. (*Glares at Angier.*) You're a magician, not a wizard – you have to get your hands dirty to achieve the impossible.

ANGIER
You sound like him.

CUTTER
(*holds up cage*)
Put your hands on the sides . . .

INT. PANTAGES THEATRE – DAY

A heavy, disinterested man slouches in the third row of the empty theatre with a newspaper – Merrit, the stage manager. Onstage, Angier energetically yanks coloured handkerchiefs from a hat and tosses them into the air. Olivia, in the glamorous, revealing costume of Magician's Assistant, darts back and forth plucking the handkerchiefs from the air.

Angier finishes with a flourish. Merrit shrugs. Angier places an ornate cage onto the table.

ANGIER

I need a volunteer.

Merrit rolls his eyes. Climbs to his feet. Angier produces a dove. Places it in the cage.

INT. ANGIER'S WORKSHOP – DAY

Now Angier is wearing the harness. He places a dove in the cage and picks it up.

Close on: hooks concealed in Angier's palm slip into catches on the bars of the cage.

CUTTER

Hang on, hang on . . .

Cutter reaches in and slips a noose around the bird's ankle . . .

There we go. Now you tell the volunteer to put his hands here . . .

Cutter places his hands on the top and bottom of the cage . . .

INT. PANTAGES THEATRE – DAY

Merrit places his hands on the top and bottom of the birdcage. Angier's hands are on the sides. Olivia reaches around Merrit to place her hands on the remaining two sides. Merrit looks up at Angier over his glasses.

MERRIT

You'd best not be intending to hurt this animal, Mr Angier.

ANGIER

Of course not.

Angier raises and lowers their hands in a rhythm . . .

And one . . . two . . . THREE!

The birdcage, and the dove, vanish.

INT. ANGIER'S WORKSHOP – DAY

Angier and Cutter have their hands on the birdcage.

ANGIER

. . . THREE!

The birdcage breaks apart, whipping up Angier's forearms, where sleeves would be, yanked by the harness. Angier smiles.

Bloody marvellous, Cutter.

CUTTER

And the best part . . .

Cutter reaches to Angier's armpit . . . pulls up the dove, hanging by its ankle, alive.

ANGIER

Thought you said I had to get my hands dirty.

CUTTER

Someday, perhaps you will. I needed to know that you can.

INT. PANTAGES THEATRE – DAY

Merrit nods, impressed, stepping backwards. Angier reaches into Merrit's pocket. Removes a dove.

MERRIT

Very nice. Very nice indeed.

Olivia packs up the props. Cutter approaches from the wings.

ANGIER
(*smiling*)

I haven't had a chance to compliment you on your beautiful theatre yet, Mr Merrit.

MERRIT

A lot more beautiful when it's full, Mr Angier.

ANGIER

Don't worry.

50

MERRIT

You all say that. Why should I worry? If your tricks don't
get 'em in, someone else's will. Maybe someone willing to
do a bullet-catch or a water escape.

CUTTER

Cheap thrills, Mr Merrit. People hoping for an accident –
and quite likely to see one, too. What would that do for
your business?

MERRIT
(shrugs)

You've got a week.

EXT. PANTAGES THEATRE – EVENING

*A line of patrons runs from the box office to the street. Posters lining
the wall behind them read:*

THE GREAT DANTON PERFORMS FEATS
OF MYSTERY AND IMAGINATION

INT. THEATRE – EVENING

Angier is performing to a good crowd. He steps forward.

ANGIER

You sir, in the hat. Could you show us your handkerchief?

*A man in the audience stands and pulls a handkerchief from his
pocket. He stares at it, confused. The audience laughs.*

MAN

This isn't mine.

ANGIER

Perhaps you'd be so good as to return it to the other man.
He has yours.

*Another man stands and pulls out a handkerchief. Applause. Angier
bows and walks quickly off the stage, past the squad of dancing girls
who run on to entertain in the break.*

INT. BACKSTAGE — EVENING

Cutter and Olivia are waiting for Angier as he comes off.

OLIVIA

I'm so nervous – I'm sorry, I'm making mistakes.

Cutter quickly removes Angier's coat . . .

ANGIER

The audience doesn't seem to be responding much.

Cutter puts the leather harness over Angier's arms . . .

CUTTER

They've seen a lot of tricks before. But not this next one.
You'll see.

Cutter checks the springs of the harness and replaces Angier's coat. He spots a Stagehand poking his head around the flies.

You! Piss off out of it!

The dancers are wrapping up.

ANGIER

Fingers crossed.

CUTTER
(*smiling*)

I'll have the champagne ready.

Angier, followed by Olivia, steps out onto the stage.

INT. STAGE — CONTINUOUS

Angier steps to the table centre stage. Pulls out the birdcage. There are one or two groans from the audience. Angier smiles as he produces a dove with a flourish.

ANGIER

You've seen this one before?

HECKLER
(*out of shot*)

Seen 'em all before, mate!

Laughter.

Well, I'll make it a little harder, shall I?

In the wings, Cutter smiles and nods at Angier's showmanship.

Two volunteers, please. A lady and a gentleman to hold this cage with me . . .

Hands go up. Olivia pulls an Elegant Lady from the audience.

I'll perform this feat in a manner never before seen by yourselves or by any other audience anywhere in the world.

Olivia brings Elegant Lady onto the stage along with a Red-Bearded Man. The audience is getting interested. Angier is on a roll . . .

Any magician can make this cage disappear . . . that's why I'll ask this good lady and fine gentleman to place their hands firmly on the cage . . .

Olivia guides Elegant Lady's hands onto the sides of the cage. Red-Beard places a hand underneath the cage.

. . . to ensure that no trickery whatsoever is employed.

Angier raises the birdcage. The audience is rapt.

Red-Beard's other hand appears on the top of the cage – it is mutilated, missing fingers.

Angier freezes – looks up at Red-Beard . . . It is Borden.

Borden smiles as he worms his little finger into the cage mechanism . . .

Snap! The cage collapses on the dove and the Elegant Lady's fingers – she screams – bird blood splatters onto the three of them – the audience goes crazy.

Borden smiles at Angier through his blood-spattered fake beard and retreats into the chaos surrounding the Elegant Lady, who is still screaming as Angier tries to free her fingers from the mechanism.

53

INT. BACKSTAGE – LATER

Angier and Cutter watch the Stagehands clear the stage.

ANGIER

I should've spotted him.

CUTTER

You had a lot of plates spinning.

Angier looks down at the harness in his hands.

ANGIER

Don't suppose they'll let us do this one again.

CUTTER

No.

ANGIER

So what's the climax of our show?

MERRIT
(*out of shot*)

Show? You don't *have* a show.

ANGIER

Mr Merrit, we have a week's engagement –

MERRIT

To perform magic – not butcher birds and break my customer's fingers! Clear out, anything here in the morning gets burned.

Cutter puts his hand on Merrit's arm.

CUTTER

Mr Merrit –

MERRIT

It's done, John. I've hired a comedian. You know I hate comedians, which should indicate the way I feel about your friend's future as a stage magician.

Cutter nods. Merrit leaves. Cutter turns to Angier.

CUTTER

There are plenty of good theatres . . . if we can come up
with another trick and change the name of the act –

ANGIER

The name stays.

Cutter sees Angier's resolve.

CUTTER

Right. Well, the new trick will have to be irresistible, then.
I've a couple of methods to try out, but we'll need a fresh
angle on the presentation.

Angier nods.

If you need inspiration, there's a technical exposition at the
Albert Hall this week. Scientists and engineers. That sort of
thing captures the popular imagination.

INT. EXHIBITION HALL – AFTERNOON

*The lobby is filled with displays and models. Angier pokes around,
looking thoroughly uninterested until he comes to an information booth
plastered with illustrations of electrical bolts.*

TICKET HAWKER

Would you like to know the future, sir? The man who will
change the world is speaking right now. Continents divided
no more. Free, clean power. The mysteries of the world
solved.

*The posters show a tall, handsome man bathed in lightning and
standing astride the world like colossus. In bold print it says:*

THE WONDERS OF 'ALTERNATING CURRENT'
N'IKOLA TESLA

INT. AUDITORIUM, EXHIBITION HALL – CONTINUOUS

*On the stage, a tall rod capped with a steel ball is transmitting a
steady, sparking stream of electricity onto a matched ball in the middle
of the audience.*

Angier stares up at the sparks as he finds a seat. Onstage, a Moderator is deep in passionate conversation with three Policemen, who are pointing at the sparking balls. Alley emerges from the wings to join the apparent debate. The audience is getting restless. The Moderator takes the stage.

MODERATOR

Ladies and gentlemen, I'm sorry, but objections have been raised concerning the safety of Mr Tesla's demonstration –

The word 'safety' unsettles the audience, who look up nervously at the giant sparks overhead.

ALLEY

Part of Thomas Edison's smear campaign against Mr Tesla's superior alternating current!

MODERATOR

Mr Alley, please! (*To audience.*) We have asked Mr Tesla to reconsider his presentation – but I'm told he refuses to appear under any such restrictions –

The rod emits a blast of electricity. The audience starts to panic, rushing from their seats.

ALLEY

It's perfectly safe!

Angier turns to look at the panic around him. He freezes, staring down the aisle.

Borden is sitting there, rapt, lit by electrical flashes.

EXT. STREET – DAY

Borden walks down the street. Angier is following him. Borden meets Sarah, pushing a pram. Borden looks down at the baby then up at Sarah.

BORDEN

I love you.

Sarah smiles.

SARAH

See? Today, it's true.

Angier watches Borden kiss his wife, then his baby.

ANGIER
(*voice-over*)

I saw happiness . . .

INT. HOTEL ROOM, COLORADO – NIGHT

Angier writing in his leather-bound journal.

ANGIER
(*voice-over*)

. . . happiness that should have been mine. But I was wrong.

Angier glances at Borden's notebook sitting on the desk.

His notebook reveals that he never had the life I envied.

Angier flips open the notebook. Staring at the coded writing.

The family life he craves one minute he rails against the next, demanding freedom. His mind is a divided one . . .

INT. PRISON CELL – DAY

Borden sits on his cot. Reading Angier's journal.

ANGIER
(*voice-over*)

His soul restless. His wife and child tormented by his fickle and contradictory nature . . .

Borden is crying. He puts the journal down and jumps to his feet, banging on the cell door.

BORDEN

Guard! Guard!!

The viewing slot slides open.

SULLEN

What do want, Professor?

BORDEN

Paper and pencil. Please.

EXT. PRISON YARD, NEWGATE PRISON – DAY

Borden sits at a table. Writing on a stack of notepaper. His arms have been unbound, but long chains runs from his elbows to where the Sullen Guard sits smoking, craning his neck to read Borden's writing.

SULLEN

Let me see.

Sullen snatches up the papers. Borden makes no move to stop him. The top sheet is a sketch of a cabinet.

I'm going to know all of the Professor's secrets.

BORDEN
(*smiling*)
Only if I teach you how to read.

Sullen mashes the papers into a ball and drops them.

SULLEN

Just stupid tricks, right? Haven't helped you get out of here – (*Tugs chains.*) Have they? Or can't you open real locks, Professor?

BORDEN

Perhaps I'm just biding my time. Perhaps one day I'll hold up my hand –

Borden produces a rubber ball in front of Sullen's face.

– get your attention. Then – (*Whispers.*) 'Are you watching closely?' . . . A magic word or two . . . and I'll be *gone* . . .

Borden vanishes the ball, but fumbles it. It drops to Borden's feet. Sullen laughs as Borden scrabbles around his ankles to retrieve the ball.

SULLEN

How'd you get so famous, then?

Borden stands.

BORDEN

Magic.

Borden turns, no longer chained. Sullen jumps to his feet to follow, but his ankle is chained to the table. The other Prisoners are laughing and cheering.

SULLEN

Oi, Borden, get back here!

Sullen fumbles with his keys as Borden takes a bow. Another Warder cracks Borden over the head with a truncheon. Sullen, now free, kicks Borden in the ribs.

Cut to:

Close on an advertisement:

THE PROFESSOR HAS
DEFIED DEATH
TO RETURN WITH A NEW SPECTACULAR!

Pull wider –

INT. ANGIER'S WORKSHOP – NIGHT

A newspaper on the make-up table. Angier sits at the mirror.

He rubs brown paste into his hair and then combs it out. Then he chooses a beard, seats it on his chin and begins to adjust it. He drops the bottle of spirit gum as he looks in the mirror and sees Olivia standing behind him.

ANGIER
(embarrassed)

I thought you'd gone.

Olivia shifts. Embarrassed.

OLIVIA

I don't really . . . have anywhere to go.

Angier slips the newspaper from the table.

ANGIER
You've been sleeping here?

OLIVIA
Cutter said it would be okay till we get another booking.
(*Beat.*) What are you doing?

ANGIER
Research. Part of a magician's job is to watch his
competition, to see what illusions they're –

OLIVIA
You're going to do something to that man, aren't you?

Olivia moves closer. Angier is quiet.

Cutter's hoping you'll let things lie. He says if Borden
thinks things are even between you then we can –

ANGIER
Even? My wife for a couple of his fingers? He has a child
now. And he's performing again. (*Bitter.*) Borden is out
there, living his life just as he always intended. As if nothing
had happened. And look at me. I'm alone. And no theatre
will touch me.

OLIVIA
Us.

Olivia moves towards him.

You're going to need a better disguise.

Olivia reaches for Angier's beard.

INT. COVENT GARDEN THEATRE – NIGHT

*Angier, almost unrecognisable as a blond, slips into the back of the
theatre, which is as rough and unwelcoming as Borden's last venue.*

*On the small raised stage, Borden works his way through the Chinese
rings with gloved hands to hide his damaged fingers. The tough crowd
is jeering at him. He finishes.*

I need a volunteer.

Angier takes a few steps towards the stage.

Borden produces a rubber ball. Tosses it to Angier.

As you can see, it's just a rubber ball. But it's not normal at all.

Angier examines the ball. Hands it back to Borden who shows no sign of recognising Angier.

Thank you.

Angier notices that two tall black cabinets are standing twenty feet apart on the stage.

(*To audience.*) You're not impressed?

Borden bounces the ball on the ground and catches it.

It's a magic ball.

Borden continues to bounce the ball on the floor. The audience looks bored, waiting for something to happen.

OLIVIA
(*voice-over*)

What happened?

INT. ANGIER'S WORKSHOP – NIGHT

Angier, still in disguise, is slumped in an armchair, drink in hand. He is smiling, remembering.

Olivia, sitting on the workbench, waits for him to continue.

OLIVIA

What happened, Robert?

ANGIER

He had a new trick.

OLIVIA

Was it good?

Angier looks at her . . .

61

INT. STRAND THEATRE – EVENING

Now it's Cutter standing in the audience, watching. Onstage, Borden bounces the ball over and over again.

> ANGIER
> (*voice-over*)
> It was the greatest magic trick I have ever seen.

Borden walks to one side of the stage and opens the door to one of the cabinets. It's empty. He closes it again and crosses the stage, bouncing the ball the whole way.

At the far cabinet, Borden repeats the process, opening the door to the empty cabinet. This time, however, he leaves the door open.

He steps forward and gently bounces the ball sideways, across the stage . . .

Borden steps into the cabinet behind him, closing the door.

With no one on stage, the audience watches as the ball continues to bounce across the stage. Bounce. Bounce. Bounce. The ball loses speed and height . . .

Just as it reaches the second cabinet, something impossible happens.

The door to the second cabinet opens and Borden steps out, catching the ball.

Cutter flinches, then studies Borden. The audience is bemused. Finally, a trickle of applause.

INT. ANGIER'S WORKSHOP – DAY

Angier is talking to Cutter. Olivia is watching.

> ANGIER
> Did they applaud when you saw it?

> CUTTER
> Not very enthusiastically.

INT. STRAND THEATRE – NIGHT

Angier, in disguise, starts clapping loudly, firmly, as if he can't help it, leading the applause.

Borden bounces the ball once again, then bows deeply. The applause peters out. Borden walks off the stage.

INT. ANGIER'S WORKSHOP – DAY

Angier turns to Cutter.

> CUTTER
>
> The trick is too good – too simple – the audience hardly knows what they've seen.

> ANGIER
>
> He's a dreadful magician.

> CUTTER
>
> He's a wonderful *magician* – he's a dreadful *showman*. He doesn't know how to dress it up, how to sell the trick.

> ANGIER
>
> How does he do it?

> CUTTER
>
> He uses a double.

> ANGIER
> (*shakes head*)
>
> It's not that simple. This is a complex illusion.

> CUTTER
>
> You think that because you don't know the method. It's a double who comes out at the end. It's the only way.

> ANGIER
>
> I've seen him perform it three times now, Mr Cutter – the Prestige is the same man –

> CUTTER
>
> It's not –

ANGIER

The same man comes out of the second cabinet. I promise you.

OLIVIA

It *is* the same man.

They both turn to look at Olivia.

He wears padded gloves to hide his damaged fingers, but if you look closely you can tell.

Angier looks at Cutter.

ANGIER

He doesn't know how to sell his trick to an audience. But I do.

CUTTER
(*nods*)

It would give us our climax.

ANGIER

The man stole my life. I'm going to steal his trick.

CUTTER

We'll have to find someone who can look like you on stage.

ANGIER

He doesn't use a double –

CUTTER
(*impatient*)

I don't *know* how Borden does it, Robert. So either you wait for Borden to retire and buy his secret, or you can listen to how I would do this trick.

Angier nods.

And the only way I know is to find you a bloody good double.

Angier smiles. Turns to Olivia, pointing to his face.

ANGIER

Take a good look – let's get out there and find me.

EXT. ROAD, PIKE'S PEAK – MORNING

Angier, swinging his cane, walks slowly up the mountain road.

EXT. TESLA'S LABORATORY – CONTINUOUS

Alley pulls the fence open with a rubber pad. They make their way down to the laboratory. Alley holds the door open, and Angier steps inside.

INT. TESLA'S LABORATORY – CONTINUOUS

The lab is illuminated by thirty-foot streamers of electrical discharge that pour from the base of the tower.

Angier stops, fearful.

                              ALLEY
     It's perfectly safe.

As Angier stares, a man begins to emerge from the very centre of the conflagration.

Bolts snap and trail after the man as he walks, in silhouette, towards Angier.

                              TESLA
     So this is the Great Danton.

Tesla emerges from the ball of electricity, dressed as if he were on his way to the opera. He brushes sparks from the sleeve of his jacket as he extends a hand to Angier.

     Mr Alley has effused about your act to me on any number
     of occasions. Something you did with pockets?

Angier returns the handshake.

                              ANGIER
     I saw your exhibition in London several years ago. I'm
     flattered you agreed to see me.

Tesla keeps hold of Angier's hand.

TESLA

Hold out your other hand.

Angier, confused, does so. Alley hands him a lightbulb, which starts to glow as he grasps its metal base.

ANGIER

What's conducting the electricity?

TESLA

Our bodies, Mr Angier, are quite capable of conducting, and indeed, producing energy.

Tesla releases Angier's hand. The bulb goes out. Alley takes it from Angier who looks at the palms of his hands.

Have you eaten, Mr Angier?

EXT. DECK, LABORATORY – MORNING

Angier, Alley and Tesla are seated around a table on a deck overlooking a spectacular view. They are eating sandwiches.

TESLA

Alley has explained that you require a very interesting device.

ANGIER

I need something impossible.

TESLA

You're familiar with the phrase 'Man's reach exceeds his grasp'? (*Off Angier's look.*) It's a lie. Man's grasp exceeds his nerve. Society tolerates only one change at a time.

Tesla looks out at the mountains.

The first time I changed the world I was hailed as a visionary. The second time I was asked politely to retire. And so here I am. (*Gestures at laboratory.*) Enjoying my 'retirement'. (*Looks at Angier.*) *Nothing* is impossible, Mr Angier. What you want is simply *expensive*.

Tesla rises, washing his hands in a basin on a side table.

66

If I built you this device, you would be presenting it only as an illusion?

ANGIER
If people thought the things I did on stage were real, they wouldn't clap – they'd scream. Think of sawing a woman in half.

Tesla nods. Considering.

TESLA
Mr Angier, the cost of such a machine –

ANGIER
Price is not an object.

TESLA
Perhaps not. But have you considered the cost?

ANGIER
I'm not sure I follow.

TESLA
I can make your machine, Mr Angier. But I can also give you some advice . . . (*Pointed.*) Go home. Forget this thing. I can recognise an obsession. As Mr Alley could tell you, I myself am given to one now and then. No good will come of it.

ANGIER
Hasn't good come of your obsessions?

TESLA
At first. But I've followed them too long. I am their slave. And one day they'll choose to destroy me.

Angier looks into Tesla's eyes.

ANGIER
If you understand an obsession, then you know you won't change my mind.

TESLA
(*smiles*)
So be it.

ANGIER

Will you build it?

TESLA

I have already begun to build it, Mr Angier. I hope you enjoy the mountain air. This will take time.

Tesla disappears into the lab.

INT. GREEN ROOM DRINKING CLUB – EVENING

The club is warm and dark. Olivia, Cutter and Angier make their way to the bar. Olivia points to the far end of the bar, to a Tramp in tattered clothing, curled over a pint.

OLIVIA
(*to Tramp*)

Gerry?

The Tramp sees Olivia, hoists himself up and spills his way down the bar to them. As he draws closer, we understand why Olivia has brought them here.

Underneath the filth and matted hair, this man is the spitting image of Robert Angier – he is played by the same actor.

Mr Angier, Mr Cutter, I would like you to meet Mr Gerald Root.

ROOT

A pleasure to meet you fine gentlemen.

Angier is staring a little too much. Root throws an arm over Angier's shoulder and draws him in.

(*Whispers.*) Would you like for me to tell you a little joke?

Angier smiles uncomfortably. Suddenly Root wraps his hands around Angier's neck and begins to throttle him.

Cutter breaks it up and pushes Root back.

(*Yelling.*) Are you laughing?

Angier is shaken. Root picks his hat up from the bar and disappears onto the street.

ANGIER

He's out of his mind.

OLIVIA

He's an out-of-work actor – of course he's out of his mind.

CUTTER

He's perfect. A little work, mind you, but when I'm done with him he could be your brother.

ANGIER

I don't need him to be my brother. I need him to be me.

CUTTER

Give me a month.

EXT. NORTH HILL – DAY

Borden escorts Sarah and their toddler, a girl, up the tree-lined street.

Borden stops abruptly. Crouches to his daughter. Reaches up and pushes a wayward lock of her hair over her ear. When his hand returns, it's holding a key.

He stands, and places the key in Sarah's hand.

SARAH

What's this for?

Borden takes her gently by the shoulders and turns her around, until she's facing a modest two-storey house.

When I asked last week you said we couldn't afford –

BORDEN

You caught me in the wrong mood.

SARAH

But you went through all the –

BORDEN

Sarah. I'm allowed to change my mind, aren't I? The act is taking off, soon we'll get into a bigger theatre. Things will work.

Sarah turns and embraces her husband.

INT. SCALA THEATRE

The auditorium is empty. Two doors in simple frames have been erected in the middle of the stage. Angier fiddles with one, opening it, walking through it. Olivia is watching.

> OLIVIA
> You walk through this one – then . . . ?

Angier stands Olivia in front of the door.

He pushes the door all the way open. Suddenly, a trap-door set into the floor pops open. Angier jumps through it –

INT. BENEATH THE SCALA STAGE – CONTINUOUS

– landing on a straw mattress positioned under the hole. He beckons to Olivia, above him.

INT. SCALA THEATRE – CONTINUOUS

Olivia gathers up her skirts and drops through the hole –

INT. BENEATH THE SCALA STAGE – CONTINUOUS

– landing beside Angier on the straw mattress.

> OLIVIA
> Oof. Couldn't you find a softer one?

> ANGIER
> (*smiles*)
> It's not for sleeping on.

Olivia looks around the below-stage area.

> OLIVIA
> And Root goes up through there?

She gestures at a lift twenty feet away with a trap-door mechanism above it. Angier nods. Olivia looks at Angier.

> It's going to be amazing, Robert.

ANGIER

It has to be. Borden's trick is getting noticed. The place was packed today.

Olivia looks at him strangely.

OLIVIA

You went and saw his show again?

Angier looks away, embarrassed.

You're becoming obsessed, Robert.

CUTTER
(*out of shot*)

Ready to meet yourself, Mr Angier?!

Angier and Olivia look up to see Cutter at the trap-door.

INT. SCALA THEATRE – MOMENTS LATER

Angier and Olivia sit in the front row. Cutter beckons Root onstage. He's been cleaned up and dressed in Angier's stage costume. He trips on his way across the stage.

ANGIER

All I have to do is keep myself stinking drunk all the time and no one will be able to tell the difference.

CUTTER

A little faith, sir. Could you favour us with a performance, Mr Root?

Root picks himself up and dusts himself off.

Suddenly, Root has become Angier. He is channelling everything from his facial expressions to his walk. Angier nods, starting to believe this might work. The illusion is perfect – till he opens his mouth.

ROOT

You would drink, too, if you knew the world half so well as I do.

Angier hops up onto stage, examining Root from different angles. Root starts aping his every movement. Olivia starts laughing. Angier is getting uncomfortable.

Did you think you were unique, Mr Angier? I have been Caesar. I have been Faust. How difficult could it possibly be to play the 'Great Danton?'

                    CUTTER
You can go back to being yourself, Root. For nothing.

Root looks challengingly at both men.

                    ROOT
I'd rather be him, for now. I find it amusing.

Root waves his hands across his chest, in the same manner that Angier does onstage. He pulls out a bottle of gin, and takes a long swallow. He jumps down to Olivia.

                    CUTTER
Root has to keep a low profile – anyone sees him, the game's up.

                    ANGIER
                  (*watching Root*)
I don't know how you do these things, Cutter. I'm not sure I want to know.

                    CUTTER
Have you thought about what we should call the trick?

                    ANGIER
No point being coy. Borden calls his trick 'The Transported Man'?

Cutter nods.

INT. LOBBY, SCALA THEATRE – EVENING

Signs on stands around the lavish, crowded lobby read:

                THE GREAT DANTON
        PERFORMS THE NEW TRANSPORTED MAN

Amongst the crowd – Fallon. Staring at the sign.

INT. SCALA THEATRE – EVENING

Angier is onstage, nearing the end of his show, smiling broadly as he pulls dozens of flowers from thin air and tosses them to the crowd. Applause fills the theatre.

The door frames are wheeled out on either side of the stage. Angier approaches the edge of the stage to address the audience with a suddenly solemn demeanour.

ANGIER

Ladies and gentlemen, much of what you've seen tonight can be termed illusions. Entertaining trifles of the sort you may have seen other magicians perform.

Angier puts on a top hat.

Alas, I cannot claim this next feat as illusion. Watch carefully – you will see no trickery, for no trickery is being employed. Merely a technique familiar to certain citizens of the orient and various holy men of the Himalayas. Indeed, some of you may be familiar with this technique, but for those of you who aren't, do not be alarmed, what you are about to see is considered safe . . .

Angier gracefully turns and heads upstage to the right-hand door, opens it, slaps it to show that it is solid.

Then strolls through, crossing the stage –

– to the other door, which he opens, slapping to show its solidity, then walking through the frame.

Angier removes his top hat and throws it high into the air. It sails back down to him and he catches it.

Angier throws the hat again, even harder this time, and it disappears up into the rafters. After a beat, it is clear it's not coming back down.

Laughter. Angier snaps his fingers and the hat is dropped back down to him. He catches it.

Angier moves to the first door and throws his hat in a high arc across the stage. He opens the door – steps behind it . . .

The second door, far across the stage, immediately opens and Angier/ Root emerges, reaching up to catch the hat.

Both doors slam shut behind him. He puts on the hat.

The audience erupts – a standing ovation, Fallon the only one in his seat as Angier/Root takes his bows.

INT. UNDER THE STAGE – CONTINUOUS

Angier, hearing the massive applause, climbs off the straw mattress, peering up through the cracks in the floorboards.

Smiling, Angier turns to the unseen audience and bows.

INT. DRESSING ROOM – EVENING

Angier, Olivia, and Cutter are celebrating their success. Empty bottles of champagne line the make-up table.

> OLIVIA
> (*toast*)

To our achievement.

They drink.

> CUTTER

The manager said he's never seen a reaction like it.

Angier smiles, rueful.

> ANGIER

At least he got to see it. I spent the ovation hidden under the stage. No one cares about the man who disappears, the man who goes into the box. They care about the man who comes out the other side.

> OLIVIA

I care about the man in the box.

Angier turns to Olivia, raises his glass.

> ANGIER

Thank you. (*To Cutter.*) Maybe we could switch before the trick. That way I could be the Prestige and Root ends up below stage.

74

CUTTER
(shakes head)
The anticipation of the trick is everything – it needs your
showmanship to build suspense. If Root opens his mouth,
it's all over – he can't introduce the trick.

ROOT
(out of shot)
Of course I can. I'm the Great Danton.

They turn. Root is lying behind a trunk, still in costume.

CUTTER
Root, you bloody fool, get that costume and make-up off
right now, anyone could walk in here!

*Cutter is slapping Root to his feet. He grabs his collar and turns to
Angier and Olivia.*

Congratulations, all.

Cutter drags Root out. Olivia slides onto the make-up table.

ANGIER
I suppose I should get some rest.

OLIVIA
Life is not full of these moments, Robbie.

Olivia pours him some more champagne.

We've worked hard for this, and we need to celebrate
properly.

*Angier looks up at her with a gentle smile. She pulls him in closer and
they kiss. She wraps her legs around him. They kiss again.*

Angier pulls back.

What's wrong? *(Softly.)* Is it your wife?

Angier shakes his head, distracted.

ANGIER
The trick isn't good enough.

Olivia stares at him.

OLIVIA

Didn't you see the audience?

ANGIER

No.

OLIVIA

Well, *they* loved it.

ANGIER

It's not as good as his trick.

OLIVIA

Borden's trick is nothing compared to ours. *He* doesn't have any style –

ANGIER

He doesn't have to spend the finale hiding under the stage.

Angier rises, turning out of her embrace.

I need to know how he does it.

OLIVIA

Why?

ANGIER

So that I can do it better.

Angier turns to her. Looks her in the eye.

I need you to go and work for him.

OLIVIA

Work for him? Are you joking?

ANGIER

You'll be my spy.

OLIVIA
(*taken aback*)

We just got our start and you want me to leave?

ANGIER

It's how we advance.

Angier moves to Olivia, placing his hands on her shoulders.

76

Think of it, Olivia . . . we've got people excited about *Cutter's* version of the trick – imagine what we could do with the *real* illusion. We'll have the greatest magic act anyone's ever seen.

                    OLIVIA
                   (*frustrated*)
He knows I work for you.

                    ANGIER
Exactly why he'll want to hire you. He'll want my secrets.

                    OLIVIA
Why would he trust me?

Angier thinks for a second. Then smiles.

                    ANGIER
Because you're going to tell him the truth.

INT. TESLA'S LABORATORY – DAY

Alley shows Angier in. Tesla is sitting, reading.

                    TESLA
You must be curious to see what so much money has bought you, Mr Angier.

Tesla rises. Leads Angier to a back corner of the room and pulls a sheet from a ten-foot-tall apparatus – the electrical machine Angier used on stage in the opening of the film.

Fitting that you should be here for the maiden voyage.

Alley fires a generator connected by thick cables to the machine. It rumbles into life, smoke pouring from its slats.

Your hat.

Angier takes off his hat and tries to hand it to Tesla. Alley intercepts the hat and lays it on a chalk hash-mark directly underneath the machine. He returns to the controls.

                    ALLEY
You might want to stand back.

No, no. It will be fine. Mr Alley, please proceed.

Without further ceremony, Alley fires the machine.

Nothing happens. Then, as they watch, the globe on top of the tripod flashes white hot. Bolts shoot out of it, wrapping themselves around the legs of the tripod. The charge reaches a frenzy and then emits a loud bang, as if it has broken the sound barrier.

Suddenly the room is still.

Tesla walks forward. Looks down into the pit.

Alley joins him at the edge of the pit. Angier, limping, is the last to arrive, looking into the pit –

– at the top hat, which hasn't moved an inch.

ANGIER

I don't understand –

Tesla stares at the hat as if trying to melt it with concentration. Alley pulls Angier away from the pit.

ALLEY

Perhaps it would be best if you left us to it. We'll see you next week?

Angier begins to protest but Alley gestures towards the door.

INT. BORDEN'S WORKSHOP – DAY

A small, disused shop off an arcade, crowded with tools, cabinetry and props, windows plastered with playbills. Borden is sitting at a workbench, sleeves rolled up, working a lathe.

Fallon enters, Olivia behind him. Borden looks back at her, turns back to the table, instinctively putting on his gloves.

OLIVIA
(*looking around*)

Interesting workshop.

BORDEN

We make do.

OLIVIA

My name is Olivia Wenscombe.

BORDEN

I know who you are. Are you here to steal the rest of my show?

Olivia sees one of the theatrical notices that litter the shop:

THE GREAT DANTON BREAKS HOUSE RECORD
WITH HIS ASTONISHING NEW TRICK

OLIVIA

No. I'm here to give your show what it's missing.

BORDEN

And what might that be?

OLIVIA

Me.

BORDEN
(to Fallon)

Wasn't I just saying that, Bernard? A woman's touch.

Fallon leaves, closing the door.

OLIVIA

I've left Angier. I want a job.

Borden sits there.

I know you have no reason to trust me –

BORDEN

Why on earth shouldn't I trust you? The mistress of my enemy.

Olivia is taken aback. Changes tack.

OLIVIA

Mr Borden –

BORDEN

Alfred.

79

OLIVIA

Alfred. I'm going to tell you the truth.

BORDEN

Ah. The truth. A slippery notion in our line of work, Miss Wenscombe.

OLIVIA

I'm here because he sent me here. He wants me to come and work for you and steal your secret.

BORDEN

What does he need my secret for? His trick is top-notch. The Great Danton vanishes and instantly reappears on the other side of the stage – mute, overweight, and, unless I'm mistaken, rather drunk.

Borden rises, moves closer to Olivia.

Tell me, Olivia. Does he like taking his bows under the stage?

Olivia meets his gaze.

OLIVIA

No. It's killing him. He's obsessed with discovering your method. He thinks of nothing else, and takes no pleasure in our success. I've had enough. There's no future with him. He sent me here to steal your secrets, but I've actually come to offer you his.

BORDEN

He has no secrets from me.

Borden stares at her, unsure.

And this is the 'truth'?

She gives Borden a challenging smile/shrug.

INT. BACKSTAGE – NIGHT

Cutter is fixing a prop mechanism. Angier approaches, in his undershirt, looks over his shoulder. Cutter glances up.

CUTTER

Best be getting changed, sir.

Angier nods. Cutter realises.

ROOT! You're late.

(*sniffs*)
And even more drunk than usual. Get yourself below stairs,
right away!

ROOT

No.

CUTTER

No?!

Root looks at Cutter with genuine malice.

ROOT

We need to have a chat, Mr Cutter.

INT. DRESSING ROOM – NIGHT

*Angier is applying his make-up. Cutter enters. Angier looks at him in
the mirror.*

ANGIER

We have a problem, Cutter.

He holds up the paper, folded to an advertisement:

PANTAGES THEATRE
FROM NEXT WEEK
THE PROFESSOR WILL DEMONSTRATE
THE ORIGINAL TRANSPORTED MAN
ACCEPT NO CHEAP IMITATIONS!!!

He'll be performing right across the street.

CUTTER

We have a bigger problem. Root.

ANGIER

Don't tell me he fell over again.

81

CUTTER

Worse. He realised he can make demands.

ANGIER

He's blackmailing us?

CUTTER

In a word, yes. I'm surprised, to be honest – it usually takes them a lot longer to figure it out.

ANGIER

How much does he want?

CUTTER

It makes no difference – we have to stop doing the trick.

ANGIER
(*wields paper*)
Stop doing the trick? Look at this.

CUTTER

Look at yesterday's. And last week's, where they called you 'London's premier stage performer', not 'magician', mind. Performer. Of any kind.

ANGIER

What's your point?

CUTTER

My point, Robert, is that you've climbed too high to get away with any kind of professional embarrassment. We're not doing any tricks we can't control.

Angier considers this. Nods. Thinking.

ANGIER

Pay him whatever he wants, for now. We keep doing the trick till Borden opens, then we'll phase it out.

INT. BENEATH THE SCALA STAGE – NIGHT

Root smokes a cigarette. Pull back to reveal he is standing on the lift beneath the stage . . .

The trap-door opens and Angier drops onto the straw mattress. He looks over to see Root finishing his cigarette.

> ANGIER
> (*hisses*)
>
> Get up there!!

Root smirks at Angier – tosses the cigarette and catapults up –

INT. STAGE, SCALA THEATRE – CONTINUOUS

– onto the stage and steps/stumbles out from behind the door to loud applause.

Root has a sloppy grin as he struts across the stage, milking the applause from every angle, blowing kisses, winking . . . loving it. He turns to Cutter in the wings. Blows him a kiss.

Cutter glares. Then turns to a Stagehand.

> CUTTER
>
> Get it down!

> ANGIER
> (*voice-over*)
>
> Cutter was always surprised how fast Root turned bad.

The Stagehand starts lowering the curtain.

INT. RESTAURANT, CLIFF HOUSE INN – DAY

Angier sits with Borden's diary.

> ANGIER
> (*voice-over*)
>
> We paid him enough to keep him in beer – you wouldn't expect him to rock the boat. Today I learned Borden's view on the episode . . .

INT. TAVERN – EVENING

The bar is dark and seedy, packed with an unpromising lot.

(*voice-over*)
. . . and his account suggests a reason.

Root is hanging precariously from his barstool, head lolling towards his empty glass. He is in his own clothes, but cleaned up to look like Angier.

A full pint arrives in front of him. Root turns to face his benefactor – Borden.

The scene will be shot two ways: with Borden and an alternate version with Borden disguised as Fallon.

Root takes several large gulps, staring at Borden. Suppresses a belch.

ROOT

To what do I owe the pleasure of this rather welcome pint of ale?

BORDEN

You are the Great Danton, aren't you?

Root gestures silence, glancing around them.

ROOT

Of course I am. But don't advertise it – I'll be mobbed with fans. (*Grins at Borden.*) And who might you be?

BORDEN

Just a humble admirer. And fellow practitioner.

ROOT

Ah, very good.

Root downs the rest of his new pint, placing the empty glass in front of Borden with an emphatic thunk.

BORDEN

Another?

ROOT

If you insist. I'm not performing tonight. Well, only one show, and, to be frank, my people pretty much run things these days.

BORDEN

You could probably do it blindfolded.

ROOT

Bloody good idea.

BORDEN

Have it.

ROOT

Thanks.

A new pint arrives. Root sips.

BORDEN

Actually, there's something I might warn you about.

ROOT

Oh?

BORDEN

Well, it's your Transported Man illusion. Now, I'm not claiming to know your method . . . but I had a similar trick in my act – and *I* used . . . (*Looks around, whispering.*) . . . a *double*.

ROOT

Oh, I see, very good.

BORDEN

At first. Then it went bad. You see, I hadn't counted on the fact that once I incorporated this bloke into my act, he had complete power over me.

ROOT

Complete power, you say?

BORDEN
(*nodding gravely*)

Well, *he* was the secret, you see. And the more successful I became, the more outrageous his demands became. He practically bankrupted me. In the end I had to stop performing the illusion completely. (*Looks at Root.*) You must be *very* careful about giving someone that power over you.

85

Root looks at Borden. Drunken wheels spinning.

> ROOT

Thanks for the warning.

INT. STAGE, SCALA THEATRE — EVENING

Angier is almost all the way through his act.

> ANGIER

... Some of you may be familiar with this technique, but for those of you who aren't, do not be alarmed, what you are about to see is considered safe ...

Angier takes his time, confident, milking it. He throws his hat into the air, catches it.

He throws it across the stage – runs at the first door, flings it open, and falls through the trap-door.

INT. UNDER THE STAGE — CONTINUOUS

Angier drops ten feet to the concrete floor. But there is nothing to break his fall.

He smashes painfully to the ground. Clutching his leg in agony, he looks up and sees someone standing on the lift twenty feet away ... Borden.

INT. STAGE — CONTINUOUS

The first door slams shut. The audience turns their attention to the second door.

The door remains closed. The hat falls gently to the floor. Silence, broken by a cough in the audience.

INT. UNDER THE STAGE — CONTINUOUS

Borden bows to Angier – the lift rockets Borden up through the stage floor.

INT. STAGE – CONTINUOUS

The second door opens, and Borden steps through, looking all around, confused, as if he doesn't know where he is. He looks back at the door, then picks up the hat . . .

INT. UNDER THE STAGE – CONTINUOUS

Angier looks at his leg – a nasty compound fracture. As he chokes on pain he can hear laughter from the audience.

INT. STAGE – CONTINUOUS

As Borden mugs with the hat, trying it on and finding it too small, something is lowered from the flies above:

Angier/Root, bound and gagged, hangs from a chain. A sign around his neck reads:

OPENING AT PANTAGES – THE PROFESSOR

Borden looks up behind him.

> BORDEN
> Great Danton, I must apologise! I simply had too much magic for my stage at the Pantages!

The Great Danton comes to rest three feet above the stage.

> Pardon my intrusion!

Borden places the top hat on Angier/Root at a jaunty angle.

Thunderous applause and laughter. Borden bows, hops down off the stage, and walks up the aisle, bowing, enjoying it all the way.

INT. STAGE – LATER

Cutter crouches over Angier, fixing a long splint to his broken leg. Behind them, Root still hangs above the stage, groaning in protest.

> CUTTER
> I don't see how Borden found him – I had him under wraps, I was careful.

ANGIER

Well, he did.

Cutter helps Angier to his feet.

CUTTER

Sir, do you think it might be her? Olivia?

Angier stops to look at Cutter.

ANGIER

No. I don't.

Cutter gestures at Root.

CUTTER

Shall we cut him down?

ANGIER

He's the Great Danton. Let him cut himself down.

EXT. PANTAGES THEATRE – NIGHT

Angier, thinly disguised, leg in long metal brace, pushes through the crowd outside the box office. The marquee:

THE PROFESSOR PERFORMS HIS MASTERPIECE
THE ORIGINAL TRANSPORTED MAN!!

And a sign –

SOLD OUT THRU SUNDAY.

SCALPER
(*out of shot*)

Need tickets, sir?

Angier turn to the Scalper. Nods.

INT. PANTAGES THEATRE – EVENING

Angier slumps into a seat at the back of the packed theatre.

Onstage: Borden works through his show with a superior degree of showmanship, even cracking a smile when called for. Working without

88

gloves, he makes much of performing tricks one-handed. He is assisted by Olivia, who looks stunning.

Borden performs the Transported Man. Borden has dressed it up with electrical apparatus. Two large glass balls transmit sparks between one cabinet and the other along bare wires.

Angier watches, anger rising as he watches Olivia's close rapport with Borden.

INT. APARTMENT – EVENING

Olivia enters into the darkened bedroom. She strikes a match and lights one of the gaslights . . .

. . . and screams as the gaslight illuminates Angier, sitting in an armchair, cane leaning against the arm of the chair.

> ANGIER
> You weren't expecting me?

> OLIVIA
> I was expecting you sooner, Robbie. Your message said 'afternoon'.

> ANGIER
> Well, it takes a bit for me to get around these days . . .

Angier raps his leg brace with his cane. Hoists himself up.

> He's taken everything from me. My wife, my career . . . now you.

> OLIVIA
> What do you mean? You sent me to –

Angier takes her by the shoulders, roughly.

> ANGIER
> I sent you to steal his secret – not to improve his act –

> OLIVIA
> That's my job –!

> ANGIER
> Or to fall in love with him!

OLIVIA

You abandoned me to him!

Angier slaps her. She shakes her head at him.

I did everything you asked.

ANGIER
(*challenging*)
Yes? Then how does he do it?!

OLIVIA

Cutter was right – it's a double.

Angier shakes his head, furious.

ANGIER

Of course Borden said that –

OLIVIA

He didn't say anything – he'd never say. I've seen things – make-up, glasses, wigs. We don't use any of it for the show, but I've found it hidden backstage.

ANGIER
(*scorn*)
It's *misdirection* – he leaves those things lying around to make you think he's using a double.

OLIVIA

All the time? He doesn't know *when* I'm looking –

ANGIER

All the time, Olivia – that's who he is, that's what it takes – he *lives* his act, don't you see?! (*Beat.*) And just because you're sleeping with him doesn't mean he trusts you.

Olivia glares at him, tears forming in her eyes.

OLIVIA

You think you can see everything, don't you?

She moves to her bed, reaching below the mattress.

But the Great Danton is a blind fool.

Olivia tosses something at Angier: a cardboard-bound notebook.

His notebook.

Angier starts leafing desperately through pages.

> ANGIER
>
> You stole it?

> OLIVIA
>
> I borrowed it for tonight. I thought you'd be able to translate some of it, but now I realise –

> ANGIER
>
> I can't.

> OLIVIA
> (*scorn*)
>
> You can't.

> ANGIER
>
> Olivia, *no one* could – (*Studies pages.*) It's a cipher – with a transposition that probably shifts every day of the diary. Even with the keyword it would take months to decode . . .

> OLIVIA
>
> And without the keyword?

> ANGIER
>
> Perhaps never. We'll see.

Angier puts the cardboard-bound notebook into his pocket. Olivia, worried, holds out her hand for the notebook.

> OLIVIA
>
> No, we won't – if I don't get that back tomorrow morning, he'll know I took it.

Angier looks at her, incredulous.

> ANGIER
>
> You can't possibly think I'd let this go? This is his diary, Olivia. All of his secrets are right here, in my hands.

> OLIVIA
> (*pleading*)
>
> Don't do this to me, Robert!

                    ANGIER
                    (*shrugs*)
          Leave him.

                    OLIVIA
          He knows where I live!

                    ANGIER
          I need to know his method.

                    OLIVIA
                    (*desperate*)
          It won't get your wife back, Robert.

                    ANGIER
          I don't care about my wife – I care about his secret!

Angier stops, realising what he said. Calms himself.

          Look, I'll go to his workshop and stage a break-in –

                    OLIVIA
          He'll know it was you –

Angier puts his hands gently on her shoulders.

                    ANGIER
          Yes, me, not you. Understand?

Olivia nods, crying. Still scared. Angier drags his leg to the door. She watches him go, torn.

                    OLIVIA
          Robert? I have fallen in love with him.

Angier looks at her, sympathetic.

                    ANGIER
          Then I know how hard this has been for you.

INT. BORDEN'S WORKSHOP – DAY

Close on: shattered glass, broken props and cabinetry.

Borden and Fallon survey the wreckage of their shop. Borden looks at Fallon.

BORDEN
Notebook?

Fallon nods. Borden sighs. Weary.

Then he's just getting started.

EXT. STAGEDOOR, PANTAGES THEATRE – EVENING

A small crowd of autograph seekers crowd the stage door. A bodyguard steps through the door and begins ushering them away as Fallon and Borden follow him through the door.

The bodyguard holds open the door to a carriage and Fallon steps up. Borden stops at the open door.

BORDEN
I'm walking tonight, gentlemen.

Fallon looks concerned.

Let him come. I don't care.

Borden doffs his hat and walks onto the crowded street.

Fallon steps down, reaches into the bodyguard's jacket and pulls out a pistol. He checks that it's loaded and slips it into his own jacket. Then he sets off after Borden.

EXT. STREETS, WEST END – EVENING

Fallon continues to follow Borden at a distance. Borden steps into a tobacconist's. Fallon stops and idles at the street corner.

As Fallon watches, across the street, another man stops. Fallon slips back around the corner and looks:

It's Angier, leaning on his cane.

Borden emerges from the tobacconist's and continues down the street, a cloud of pipe smoke drifting after him.

Fallon waits for Angier to set off after Borden, then follows both men from a distance.

Borden crosses to the same side of the street as Angier. Fallon picks up his pace and tries to cross the street but is held up for a second by passing traffic.

As he reaches the other side, Borden is gone, but he sees Angier disappearing down an alleyway.

EXT. ALLEY – CONTINUOUS

Fallon rounds the corner and stops. The alleyway is empty – he has lost them. Finally, he sees an open, darkened doorway towards the end of the alleyway.

INT. HALLWAY – CONTINUOUS

Fallon stops at the doorway, his gloved hand gripping the door frame.

Angier stands at the other end of the hallway, watching him.

Fallon takes a step towards him and crashes through the rotten floor to the basement below.

INT. BASEMENT – CONTINUOUS

Fallon drops heavily into an almost-vertical open coffin.

Disoriented, Fallon just glimpses Cutter drop the lid into place, shutting him in. Cutter starts nailing it down.

A gunshot tears through the lid of the box. Cutter falls back, but is caught by Angier.

Angier rolls Cutter off to one side. He is clutching at a bloody wound on his arm.

CUTTER

I'll live. (*To coffin.*) You saved me the trouble of making you an air hole!

Angier picks up the hammer and continues nailing.

EXT. HIGHGATE CEMETERY – MORNING

Borden picks his way through the overgrown cemetery. He hears a knocking and turns:

Angier is behind him, rapping on a broken headstone with the head of his cane.

> BORDEN
>
> I'm impressed.

> ANGIER
>
> Why's that?

> BORDEN
>
> You're finally getting your hands dirty. This is what a good trick costs, Angier. Risk. Sacrifice.

> ANGIER
>
> The sacrifice, I'm afraid, is all going to be yours. Unless you give me what I want.

> BORDEN
>
> Which is?

> ANGIER
>
> Your secret.

Borden tries to gauge Angier's expression.

> BORDEN
>
> My secret?

> ANGIER
>
> Your method for the Transported Man. Fallon wouldn't tell me. In fact, he doesn't talk at all.

> BORDEN
> (*shrugs*)
>
> You have my notebook.

> ANGIER
>
> Useless without the keyword.

Angier pulls a sheaf of writing paper and a pencil stub from his pocket. He offers them to Borden.

Write down your method, Mr Borden. Describe it in full.

Borden takes the paper and pencil and stares Angier in the eye, gauging him.

Beat.

Borden writes a single word on the top page and folds it up.

I want the *whole method*, not the keyword – I don't even know if the secret is in your notebook.

Borden looks at Angier with a glint in his eye.

                    BORDEN
The keyword is the method.

Angier reaches for the folded paper, which Borden lifts out of reach.

Where is my *ingénieur*?

Angier pulls a shovel free from a pile of dirt beside him. He stakes it into a fresh pile of dirt in front of Borden. Borden looks at Angier, concerned.

Is he alive?

Angier plucks the folded paper from Borden's hand.

                    ANGIER
How fast can you dig?

Angier moves away through the headstones, leaning heavily on his cane. Borden begins to dig.

INT. HOSPITAL – DAY

Cutter is slumped in a chair by the wall, his arm bandaged. He smiles up at Angier, who sits down next to him.

                    ANGIER
How's the arm?

                    CUTTER
Still attached. Did you get your answer?

Angier holds up the folded paper.

ANGIER

Our answer, Cutter. I haven't looked yet, I wanted you to
share this.

Cutter looks curiously at Angier.

CUTTER

I already know how he does it, Robert. The same way he
always has, the same way *we* do. You just *want* it to be
something more.

Angier looks at Cutter, uneasy.

ANGIER

Well, let's find out, shall we?

*Angier opens the piece of paper. A large grin spreads across his face.
He turns it to Cutter – it reads* TESLA.

Cutter frowns, confused.

CUTTER

What does it mean?

ANGIER
(*excited*)

It means, Cutter, that we have a journey ahead of us. To
America.

Cutter watches Angier's excitement. Awkward.

CUTTER

Robert, listen to me. (*Gentle, but definite.*) Obsession is a
young man's game, I can't follow you any farther in this.

*Angier looks at Cutter, uncomprehending. He considers saying
something. Stops. Restrains himself.*

ANGIER

Then the rest is up to me.

INT. ELEGANT RESTAURANT – EVENING

*Sarah sits by herself at a table for two. Borden enters with a swagger,
Olivia beside him, Fallon behind. The Maître D' hurries over,
signalling Waiters. Sarah looks up, uncomfortable.*

97

SARAH

I didn't know we'd be joined for dinner.

BORDEN

Absolutely. We're celebrating.

The Waiters spirit another table and chairs to join Sarah's. Borden pulls out a chair for Olivia.

SARAH

Miss Wenscombe. Mr Fallon.

Olivia smiles cheerfully. Fallon nods, embarrassed.

BORDEN
(*to Wine Waiter*)

Champagne. Your finest.

SARAH

What are we celebrating, dear?

BORDEN

Well, we've hit upon a new trick, haven't we, Fallon?

OLIVIA

What trick, Freddy?

SARAH
(*brittle*)

Yes, 'Freddy'. What trick?

The Waiter presents a bottle of champagne. Borden nods without looking at it.

BORDEN
(*loud*)

I'm going to *bury* myself alive. Every night. Then someone's going to come along and dig me up!

Other diners are glancing over. The Waiter uncorks the bottle with a muffled pop and pours champagne into Borden's glass.

SARAH
(*to Waiter*)

I'm not sure my husband needs –

BORDEN

Who are you to tell me that?!

Awkward silence. Olivia shifts in her seat.

OLIVIA

Perhaps –

SARAH

Perhaps, Mr Fallon, you might escort Miss Wenscombe
home. My husband's being a bore, I see no reason for the
two of you to suffer as well.

Fallon is on his feet, pulling back Olivia's chair.

OLIVIA

Goodnight, Mrs Borden. Goodnight, Freddy.

They leave. Borden glares at his wife.

SARAH

'Freddy'?

BORDEN

It's my name.

SARAH

Not at home.

BORDEN

I'm not always at home.

Sarah is clearly on the verge of tears.

SARAH

Alfred, why are you being like this?

Borden, seeing her distress, softens.

BORDEN

Sarah, I had a terrible ordeal today. I thought I'd lost
something very precious to me.

SARAH

What?

Borden looks at her, speechless. Shrugs helplessly.

I see. More secrets.

                    BORDEN
Secrets are my life, Sarah. Our life.

Sarah brushes away a tear.

                    SARAH
When you're like this, Alfred, I'm not seeing the real you.
You're treating me like your audience. Performing. I can't
live with that.

Borden just sits there. Offering nothing.

EXT. CLIFF HOUSE INN – DAY

*Angier walks up to the hotel. A motor car is parked in front, and two
men are unloading it. One of the men stares at Angier as he enters the
hotel.*

INT. CLIFF HOUSE INN

Angier walks to the reception desk.

                    ANGIER
I thought I had the place to myself.

                    MANAGER
Unexpected guests. (*Looks out the window at the men.*) Not
very polite. A lot of questions. At first I thought they might
work for the government.

                    ANGIER
No?

                    MANAGER
                 (*lowers voice*)
Worse. They work for Thomas Edison.

Angier stares out the window at the men unloading equipment.

INT. HOTEL ROOM, COLORADO – CONTINUOUS

Angier sits at the desk, deciphering Borden's diary.

> BORDEN
> (*voice-over*)
> Today, a most curious development . . .

INT. BORDEN'S WORKSHOP – DAY

Borden turns to see Fallon show in Olivia.

> BORDEN
> (*voice-over*)
> His assistant came to us with a proposition . . .

They start to speak as Borden's voice-over continues.

> Obviously Angier has sent her, and told her to admit as much . . .
>
> (*To Olivia.*) Tell me, Olivia. Does he like taking his bows under the stage?

Olivia meets his gaze.

> OLIVIA
> No. It's killing him. He's obsessed with discovering your method. He thinks of nothing else, and takes no pleasure in our success. I've had enough. There is no future with him. He sent me here to steal your secrets, but I've actually come to offer you his.

> BORDEN
> He has no secrets from me.

Borden stares at her, unsure.

> This is the 'truth' you spoke of?

She gives him a sly smile.

> OLIVIA
> No. This is what he told me to tell you.

Beat.

The truth is that I loved him. And stood by him. And he sent me to you like he'd send a stagehand to pick up his shirts. (*Looks him in the eye.*) I hate him for that.

They sit there in silence, appraising each other.

BORDEN

I can spot Angier's methods from the back of the theatre. What could you possibly have to offer me?

Olivia smiles, moves to Borden, reaching for his gloved hand. Borden flinches, surprised.

OLIVIA

You may know how he does his tricks . . . but you can't understand why no one can see that yours are better.

She tenderly peels off his padded glove revealing his mutilated hand.

You hide this. I had to look closely to spot it when you performed the Transported Man. (*Looks into his eyes.*) But this makes you *unique* . . . it shows the audience that you aren't using a double. You mustn't hide it, you must display it proudly . . . (*Looks at hand.*) I'm sure it takes great skill to perform illusions with one good hand.

BORDEN
(*quiet*)

It does.

OLIVIA

Then let people know. You can be so much *more* than he is. I can show you how.

Borden looks into her eyes.

BORDEN
(*voice-over*)

I think she is telling the truth.

INT. BEDROOM, BORDEN'S WORKSHOP – NIGHT

Borden and Olivia are in bed together. It is raining outside.

He watches her get out of bed and moves to the window to smoke a cigarette.

> BORDEN
> (*voice-over*)
>
> I think we cannot trust her. But I love her. I need her. *We* need her.
>
> (*To Olivia.*) How could he send you away? He must be blind, deaf and dumb.

She smiles quietly at this.

> OLIVIA
>
> Robbie's blinded by his jealousy. He'd do *anything* for your secret. Sending me away was the least of it.

Borden considers this.

> BORDEN
> (*voice-over*)
>
> Trust is not the point – love is the point . . . who have we ever trusted? To open myself to such a relationship . . .

EXT. NARROW ALLEYWAY – DAY

Olivia makes her way past crowded market stalls.

> BORDEN
> (*voice-over*)
>
> . . . to the dangers of such an affair . . . I need assurances of fidelity. Of love.

Fallon is shadowing her from a distance.

> But how to be sure when truth is layered like the skin of an onion? I know a way . . . she must help me rid ourselves of Angier. It is the only way to know her mind.

INT. HOTEL ROOM, COLORADO – DAY

Angier looks up from Borden's diary. Pale. He flips pages and pages forward to the last entry . . .

BORDEN
(*voice-over*)

Today my mistress proves her truthfulness. Not to me,
you understand. I have been convinced since she led me
to Root . . . today, Olivia proves her love for me to *you*,
Angier.

Angier looks up from the notebook. Mind reeling.

Yes, Angier. She gave you this notebook at my request. Yes,
she led me to Root, and yes, Tesla is merely the key to my
diary, not to my trick. Did you really think I would part
with my secret so easily after so much? Goodbye, Angier,
may you find solace for your thwarted ambition back in
your American home.

Angier stares at the pages, unblinking. Jumps to his feet . . .

EXT. TESLA'S LABORATORY – DAY

Angier strides up to the fence.

ANGIER

TESLA!

Nothing.

TESLA!!

*Angier takes his cane and starts running its metal tip across the
electrified fence – causing sparking and crackling.*

ALLEY, GET OUT HERE AND LET ME IN!!

Alley emerges from the building, confused.

INT. TESLA'S LABORATORY – DAY

Alley opens the door – Angier bursts in past him, enraged.

ANGIER

I've been played for a fool!

ALLEY

Who by?

ANGIER

Tesla never made a machine like the one I asked for.

ALLEY

We never said he had.

ANGIER

You let me *believe* that he had, Alley! You stole my money because your funding was cut off – you've been shooting sparks at my top hat, laughing at me all along while you use my money to stave off ruin. I've seen Edison's men –

ALLEY

Where?

ANGIER

In the hotel. I've every mind to bring them up here myself.

TESLA
(*out of shot*)

That would be unwise, Mr Angier.

Tesla is holding a cage containing a large black cat.

It is true, sir, that you are our one remaining financier. But we have not stolen your money . . .

ALLEY

Sir, my cat?

Tesla silences Alley with a tiny glance.

TESLA

When I told you I could make your machine I spoke the simple truth.

ANGIER

Then why isn't the machine working?

Tesla gives Angier the slightest of smiles.

TESLA

Because exact science, Mr Angier, is not an exact science.

The machine simply does not operate as expected. It requires further examination.

ANGIER

Where did my top hat go?

ALLEY

Nowhere.

Alley points to the top hat, which is sitting on a workbench.

We've tried the damn thing a dozen times. The hat went nowhere.

Tesla looks at Angier with formidable calm.

TESLA

We need to try a different material. It may provoke a different result.

Tesla opens the cage and points the open end at Alley. Alley reluctantly reaches into the cage and pulls out the terrified cat. He jumps down into the pit and secures the animal by its collar to an eye-hook sunk into the ground.

ALLEY

You are responsible for whatever happens to this animal, Doctor.

Alley pulls himself out of the pit, and Tesla charges the generator.

The cat stares up at the machine around it and hisses.

Tesla fires the machine. As before, large bolts spew from the head of the machine, down towards the unseen cat. The machine builds to a deafening roar, then sputters out.

Silence. The three men begin edging towards the pit.

Suddenly, a terrifying screech. The cat is still there, still tied to the hook. Alley starts to free the cat. Angier looks up at Tesla with contempt.

ANGIER

I hope that whatever you were really doing with my money was more worthwhile, Mr Tesla.

Angier turns, limping towards the open side door. Tesla stares at the cat, perplexed. Suddenly, the cat bursts free of Alley and rockets towards the door.

EXT. TESLA'S LABORATORY – CONTINUOUS

As Angier walks towards the woods, the cat shoots past.

EXT. FOREST – CONTINUOUS

Angier walks through the trees. Suddenly, he hears a horrible screeching.

He stops at the opening of a tiny glade, ten feet across.

Two identical black cats are fighting viciously. He tries to separate the two animals, and succeeds in grabbing one. The other cat races off.

Angier takes a few steps after it, then freezes, staring at –

– top hats. Clustered in a small glade. The first cat slinks its way through them.

The second black cat jumps from Angier's hands – races into the glade, hissing, spitting, chasing the first cat into the woods beyond.

Angier is left alone in the clearing, staring at the pile of dozens of identical top hats. He turns in the direction of the lab.

> ANGIER
>
> Alley!!

EXT. PORCH, TESLA'S LABORATORY – DAY

The top hats are in a pile on the deck. Tesla is at the table, measuring two hats with a pair of callipers. Angier and Alley are watching.

> ANGIER
> So the machine was working?

> ALLEY
> I never bothered to check the calibration. The hat never moved.

TESLA

These things never quite work as you expect them to, Mr Angier. That's one of the principal beauties of science.

Tesla looks carefully at the hat in his hands. It has a tiny tear on the inside of the brim. He picks up another hat. It has the same tear.

I'll need a couple of weeks to iron out the – (*Looks at hats.*) – problems with the machine. We'll send word when it's ready.

Angier, still dazed, takes his cane and heads for the door.

Don't forget your hat.

Angier stops and looks at the pile of hats.

ANGIER

Which one is mine?

TESLA

They are all your hat, Mr Angier.

Tesla smiles at him.

INT. BORDEN'S HOUSE – DAY

Borden's daughter, Jess, now four, runs into the room and tries to hop up into his lap. Laughing, he helps her up.

JESS

Are we going to the zoo this afternoon, Daddy?

BORDEN

Daddy's got some business this afternoon.

JESS

But you promised.

BORDEN

Did I?

Jess nods at him, solemnly.

Then go to the zoo we shall.

Borden holds the newspaper open for her to look at.

(*Gestures to newspaper.*) Who's that?

A large advertisement features a picture of Borden: 'The Professor – England's Premiere Magician!'

JESS

That's you, Daddy.

Borden picks the girl off of his lap and stands.

BORDEN

Daddy has some errands to run. I'll be back before you know it, so get ready.

Borden walks to the door. As he does, Sarah enters, avoiding his eyes, then ducking him as he tries to kiss her.

She reaches for the sherry decanter. He watches her pour. Sarah looks at him, eyes red from crying.

SARAH

We each have our vices.

Borden moves to her, gentle concern in his eyes.

BORDEN

Sarah. Whatever you may think, your only competition for my affections is my little girl. I love you. I will always love you, and you alone.

She looks into his eyes. Fascinated.

SARAH

You mean it today.

BORDEN

Absolutely.

SARAH

That makes it so much harder when you don't.

She turns from him. Borden watches her sadly. Leaves.

EXT. STREET – AFTERNOON

Borden turns off the main street and into a narrow passageway.
Another man is there – Fallon.

Fallon hands Borden a folded piece of paper. He studies it.

> BORDEN
>
> More shopping. She does like the smell of money, doesn't
> she?

Fallon looks away. Borden tears up the paper.

> The little lady wants to visit the zoo, I thought you could
> take her. I'll do it tomorrow, if not. (*Looks at his feet.*) Sarah
> . . . she knows. At least, she knows things aren't right.
> (*Looks at Fallon, pleading.*) Help me with her. Try and
> convince her that I love her. Please.

Borden, embarrassed, pats Fallon on the shoulder and makes off down
the path. Fallon sets off in the opposite direction.

INT. OLIVIA'S APARTMENT

Olivia, barely wearing a dressing gown, answers the door to Borden.
She pulls him in, trying to draw him into a kiss, but he backs away.

> OLIVIA
>
> What is it, Freddy?

> BORDEN
>
> Please don't call me that. It's nothing, just . . . sometimes
> things seem . . . wrong.

Olivia looks at him. Cold.

> OLIVIA
>
> Freddy, I've told you before. When you're with me, you're
> with me. Leave your family at home where they belong.

> BORDEN
>
> I'm trying, Olivia. Please.

> OLIVIA
>
> I'll get dressed.

Borden watches her move down the hall.

(*Out of shot.*) I saw Fallon hanging around again.

Olivia comes back in, half-dressed.

There's something about him I don't trust.

> BORDEN
You trust me? (*Off her look.*) Then trust Fallon – he protects the things I care about.

EXT. CLIFF HOUSE INN – MORNING

Angier walks out from the lobby. The two men he saw before are loading up their automobile. Smiling, laughing.

EXT. ROAD, PIKE'S PEAK – MORNING

The coach pulls to a stop. Angier and the driver look up.

A plume of smoke is rising from further up the hill.

EXT. CLEARING, PIKE'S PEAK – MOMENTS LATER

Angier rounds the bend in the road and comes into view of the laboratory. He freezes.

The fence has been torn down. Beyond it, the lab has been burned to the ground. The metal tower is in smouldering pieces. Everything else is gone.

Angier notices a piece of metal lying in the road near him, and, using his cane, flips it over. It's Alley's sign warning trespassers to keep out.

INT. ANGIER'S ROOM, CLIFF HOUSE INN – DAY

Angier studies a picture of Julia, then puts it in the top of his packed suitcase.

INT. LOBBY, CLIFF HOUSE INN – MORNING

The Bellboys wrestle with Angier's cases as Angier walks to the reception desk. The Manager smiles up at him.

> MANAGER
>
> We're sorry to see you go, Mr Angier.

Angier takes out his wallet and begins laying down bills.

> We were sorry to see Mr Tesla leave as well. He was very good to Colorado Springs. A very generous man.

Angier smiles up at him, absently and begins to leave.

> Mr Angier?

Angier turns.

> I didn't feel it was necessary to tell the other men about the box.

Angier stops.

> ANGIER
>
> What box?

The Manager smiles.

INT. HALLWAY, CLIFF HOUSE INN – MORNING

Angier follows the Manager down a hallway.

> MANAGER
>
> We never use these rooms in the off-season. It's a shame.

The Manager stops at a set of double doors and unlocks them. He pushes them open and ushers Angier through.

INT. BALLROOM, CLIFF HOUSE INN – CONTINUOUS

Angier steps into the massive, elegant room.

Standing on the dance floor is an enormous shipping crate. Stencilled on one side COLORADO SPRINGS.

Angier walks up to the huge crate, awestruck.

An envelope addressed to him has been stuck to the front. Angier opens it and begins to read.

> TESLA
> (*voice-over*)
>
> My dear Angier, I apologise for leaving without saying goodbye . . .

EXT. TESLA'S LABORATORY – NIGHT – FLASHBACK

Under cover of night, a group of figures ransack the laboratory.

> TESLA
> (*voice-over*)
>
> But I seem to have outstayed my welcome in Colorado.

The figures begin setting fire to the sides of the laboratory.

> The truly extraordinary is not permitted in science and industry. Perhaps you'll have more luck in your field, where people are happy to be mystified. You will find what you were looking for in this box . . .

INT. ABANDONED THEATRE – DAY

The open crate sits empty at the side of a derelict stage. Angier, in shirt sleeves, is running cables to the machine, which is standing centre stage.

> TESLA
> (*voice-over*)
>
> Alley has written you a thorough set of instructions. I add only one suggestion on using the machine –

EXT. COLORADO SPRINGS – NIGHT – FLASHBACK

Alley holds open the door to a coach. Tesla steps up into it and looks back from the coach's open door, up the mountain.

TESLA
(voice-over)

– destroy it. Drop it to the bottom of the deepest ocean.

High on the mountain, the laboratory is ablaze.

Such a thing will bring you only misery.

Tesla folds himself into the coach, shutting the door as it moves off down the mountain.

INT. ABANDONED THEATRE – DAY

Angier moves to one side of the stage where he makes a hash-mark with a piece of chalk.

ANGIER
(voice-over)

Tesla's warning is as unheeded as he knew it would be. Today I tested the machine . . .

He loads a gun and places it next to the machine.

Taking precautions in case Tesla hadn't ironed out the kinks in its operation . . .

Angier throws the switch. The machine groans into life – sparking and glowing as it gets up to full power.

. . . if it went wrong I would not want to live like that for long . . .

Angier closes his eyes for an instant, listening to its power, then throws himself into the machine. He is consumed by light . . .

White screen.

But here, at the Turn, I must leave you, Borden . . .

The white becomes handwriting on a page and we are –

INT. PRISON CELL – DAY

Borden stares at Angier's journal in disbelief.

ANGIER

(*voice-over*)

Yes, you, Borden. Sitting there, in your cell, reading my diary. Awaiting your death. For my murder.

Borden slams the journal shut. Staring at it.

EXT. PRISON YARD, NEWGATE PRISON – DAY

Borden stands at the fence again.

OWENS

Lord Caldlow was happy to hear that you'd reconsidered his offer.

BORDEN

Angier's journal, the 'gesture of good faith'? It's a fake.

OWENS

(*surprised*)

I assure you it's not.

BORDEN

It has to be – it refers to events that happened after his death.

OWENS

Clever predictions, I'm sure. The provenance of the journal is clear and under no doubt. It's written in Angier's own hand, of which we have numerous examples. (*Looks at Borden.*) What makes you think it's a fake?

Borden looks away, uncomfortable.

BORDEN

It doesn't matter.

Borden leans forward and stuffs rolled papers through the fence. Owens takes them carefully.

My tricks. All of them.

OWENS

Including the Transported Man? Lord Caldlow will be very pleased.

BORDEN

No he won't. They're not complete – you only have the
Pledge and Turn for each.

Owens leafs through the papers, annoyed.

OWENS

Without the Prestige for each trick these are worthless.

BORDEN

You'll get the rest after you bring my daughter here.

Owens looks at Borden.

I want to say goodbye.

INT. BORDEN'S HOUSE – NIGHT

*Jess sits at the foot of the stairs, listening to her parents shout at each
other in the living room. She is crying.*

BORDEN
(*out of shot*)

Stop it! Just stop it!

SARAH
(*out of shot*)
Deny it all you want – I know!

INT. LIVING ROOM, BORDEN'S HOUSE – CONTINUOUS

*Sarah is wild, eyes red, hair a mess. Utterly distraught. Borden is
trying to calm her.*

BORDEN
Sarah, it's not true! I've told you Olivia means nothing to
me!

SARAH
I'll go to her! I know what you really are, Alfred!

BORDEN
(*quietly firm*)
Sarah. You can't do that.

116

INT. HALLWAY, BORDEN'S HOUSE – CONTINUOUS

Jess looks up. Fallon is standing above her. Listening.

> SARAH
> (*out of shot*)
> I'll do what I have to!

Jess reaches up a hand. Fallon takes it in his.

> BORDEN
> (*out of shot*)
> Sarah, you can't talk like this!

INT. LIVING ROOM, BORDEN'S HOUSE – CONTINUOUS

Sarah turns to face Borden. Desperate.

> SARAH
> I can't *live* like this!

> BORDEN
> (*angry*)
> What do you want from me!

Sarah pauses. Catches her breath.

> SARAH
> (*quiet*)
> I want you to be honest with me. No tricks, no lies, no
> secrets.

Borden calms. Looks into her eyes. Nods.

> Do you love me?

Borden looks into her eyes. Sincere.

> BORDEN
> Not today.

Sarah takes this in. Borden watches, helpless.

> SARAH
> (*whispers*)
> Thank you.

Borden watches her turn away from him.

INT. HALLWAY, BORDEN'S HOUSE – CONTINUOUS

Jess reaches up to Fallon with her other hand. He takes her gently in his arms. We stay on Jess's tear-stained face over Fallon's shoulder as he carries her up the stairs.

INT. BORDEN'S WORKSHOP – MORNING

Close on a poster: Borden, in costume, looking intense:

THE PROFESSOR – MASTER OF DARK FORCES.

As we pull back we hear a gentle creaking . . .

Pull back past a hanging pair of feet, one shoe missing . . . wider shot shows us that it is Sarah, hanging by her neck from a beam in the middle of the shop. Gently swinging.

INT. PUBLIC HOUSE – DAY

Cutter is finishing his meal at the bar. He goes to take a swig from his pint and freezes – at the bottom of the glass: a playing card. He looks around the bar. No one he recognises. He reaches into the glass.

Cutter pulls out the card – an address is written up one side.

EXT. ABANDONED THEATRE – DAY

Cutter walks along labyrinthine streets. Stops at an abandoned theatre. He looks up at the building, then enters.

INT. ABANDONED THEATRE – DAY

Cutter makes his way past the tattered box office and into the derelict auditorium.

In the middle of the room is the crate. Cutter stands and stares at it.

> MALE VOICE
> (*out of shot*)

Who's there?

Cutter turns. A Stagehand. His eyes are solid white. The man is clearly blind.

CUTTER

I – I'm looking for an old friend –

ANGIER

(*out of shot*)

I heard about a booking . . .

Cutter turns. Angier is behind him, leaning on his cane. Beside Angier is a second Blind Stagehand.

Nice little theatre. Good up-and-coming magician.

CUTTER

You came back.

ANGIER

It's good to see you, John.

Cutter sizes Angier up. Looks around the theatre.

CUTTER

Good rehearsal space. Blind stagehands. I like it – (*Knowing smile.*) You always had an eye for publicity.

Angier sits in one of the stalls. Cutter follows suit.

ANGIER

I need your help, John. My last show. A limited engagement.

CUTTER

Your *last* show?

ANGIER

A wise man once told me that obsession was a young man's game. I'm almost done. One thing left . . . (*Points at crate.*) The *real* Transported Man.

Cutter stares at the crate.

CUTTER

You want to design a show around it?

ANGIER

I don't want you backstage, I need you front of house, managing.

Cutter considers this. Uncertain.

I need you calling in any favours and connections you have left to get us the right booking for the run.

CUTTER

What sort of booking are you after?

ANGIER

The sort that Borden can't ignore.

Cutter looks at Angier. Nods.

EXT. ABANDONED THEATRE – DAY

A long, expensive carriage creeps to a halt outside the abandoned theatre, and the confused driver pulls over.

DRIVER

This is the address, Mr Ackerman.

The carriage opens, an imposing man in his fifties steps out, looks the place up and down, then heads inside.

INT. ABANDONED THEATRE – CONTINUOUS

The man enters the auditorium and stares down at the brightly lit stage.

Cutter moves quickly up the aisle, hand outstretched.

CUTTER

It's an honour to see you again, sir.

Ackerman shakes Cutter's hand.

ACKERMAN

When you said you only wanted to show me one trick it piqued my interest.

CUTTER

It's a very special trick, Mr Ackerman.

Angier has appeared.

ANGIER

Pleased to meet you, Mr Ackerman.

ACKERMAN

Likewise, I'm sure. Let's get on, shall we?

Angier smiles.

CUTTER
(*down to stage*)

Turn it on, please.

After a moment, the machine sparks into life. Electric bolts cascade from the globe and splash on the stage.

ACKERMAN

Very pretty.

Angier smiles at Cutter and heads back down to the stage. He steps into the machine and disappears.

The machine sputters out and is silent.

That's it, Cutter? He simply disappears? That's not a trick. He has to come back. There has to be a –

VOICE
(*out of shot*)

– a Prestige?

ACKERMAN

Exactly –

Ackerman begins to turn around – then stops.

Angier is standing directly behind him.

Ackerman is dumbfounded. He looks back down at the stage.

(*Quiet, haunted.*) Pardon me. It's very rare to see . . . *real* magic. It's been many years since I've seen . . .

Ackerman steadies himself.

> ANGIER
> Are you interested in helping us?

> ACKERMAN
> (*nods*)
> Yes. But you'll have to dress it up a little. Disguise it. Give
> them enough reason to doubt it.

INT. STAGE MANAGER'S OFFICE, SCALA THEATRE – DAY

*Merrit sits eating a sandwich. The door to his office opens and
Ackerman strides in. Merrit struggles to his feet.*

> MERRIT
> (*surprised*)
> Mr Ackerman. When they said . . . I didn't think you'd be
> here *in person*.

Ackerman sits without being asked to.

> ACKERMAN
> I have an act for your venue.

> MERRIT
> (*flustered*)
> Well, of course, sir . . . But I'm afraid I'm booked. The
> Moscow Ballet. They're playing through next year.

> ACKERMAN
> Get rid of them. This is a magical act. An excellent one.
> I believe you booked his first engagement several years ago.
> The Great Danton.

> MERRIT
> You really want me to –

Ackerman stands.

> I'll do it. Of course.

Ackerman picks up a pen and paper from Merrit's desk.

ACKERMAN

There will be one hundred performances. No more, no less.
Five performances a week. No matinees, no weekends.

Ackerman scribbles onto the paper and hands it to Merrit.

(*Smiles.*) And *that's* what you'll be charging for each ticket.
Good day.

*Ackerman sweeps out of the room, leaving Merrit dumbfounded,
staring at the scrap of paper in his hands.*

INT. RESTAURANT — DAY

*Olivia and Borden are seated across from each other, finishing their
meal. Olivia watches Borden eat.*

OLIVIA

You haven't spoken about her, Freddy. Not once.

BORDEN

Who?

OLIVIA

Don't be cruel.

BORDEN

Why would I talk about her to you?

OLIVIA

Because she was part of your life and now she's gone.

Borden says nothing.

She wanted to meet me the day before she killed herself.
Said she had something to tell me about you. (*Looks away.*)
I was such a coward, I couldn't bring myself to face her.
(*Looks at Borden.*) What would she have said, I wonder?

BORDEN
(*snaps*)

You want the truth about me, Olivia?

She nods, wary.

I never loved Sarah.

123

OLIVIA
(*appalled*)
You married her, had a child with her –

BORDEN
Part of me loved her. But part of me didn't. The part that found *you*. The part that's sitting here now. I love *you*. *That* is the truth that matters.

Olivia tosses her napkin on her plate.

OLIVIA
You could be sitting in some other restaurant talking to some other woman about me that way. It's inhuman to be so cold.

Borden watches her rise from the table. She looks at him.

By the way, have you seen who's opened at the Pantages?

Borden shakes head.

The Great Danton.

BORDEN
He's back?

OLIVIA
After two years. And he has a new trick. They're saying it's the best that London's ever seen.

Borden cannot hide his reaction.

If you could see the look on your face, Professor. You should go to him – you *deserve* each other.

Olivia smiles at him and leaves.

INT. LOBBY, SCALA THEATRE – EVENING

Signs on stands throughout the packed lobby:

THE GREAT DANTON PRESENTS
THE REAL TRANSPORTED MAN
100 PERFORMANCES ONLY

INT. SCALA THEATRE – EVENING

Borden, in disguise, takes his seat halfway along the aisle.

The lights dim. Curtains rise on a simple stage. Bare except for a water-filled glass tank.

Borden stiffens in his seat, perplexed.

Angier limps onto the stage. Addresses the audience.

> ANGIER
> Ladies and gentlemen, my first trick of the evening is one that involves considerable risk. (*Removes his coat.*) Anyone in the audience who would be irrevocably damaged by seeing a man drown should leave *now*, for when I tell you that the young lady who taught me this illusion actually died performing it, you will understand the seriousness of the dangers involved.

Borden watches the hook descend from the flies. Remembering.

Insert cut: Borden stares as Angier desperately brushes the water from Julia's face.

INT. SCALA THEATRE – LATER

Angier steps forward as another curtain is drawn up behind him, revealing Tesla's machine.

> ANGIER
> In my travels I have seen the future, and it is a strange future indeed. The world is on the brink of new and terrifying possibilities.

The audience recoils in terror as the machine is started and bolts fly from it. Smoke drifts over the audience.

Borden inches forwards in his seat. Angier stands in front of the machine, silhouetted by the frenzy of electricity behind him. He tosses his cane to his assistant and steps into the machine.

The audience screams as large bolts blast from the machine and wrap themselves around Angier's arms and legs.

Borden is watching very carefully. Angier is almost impossible to see as the machine builds to a climax, but, just before it does, Borden catches a glimpse of Angier's body falling through a trap-door.

The machine sputters out. Angier has disappeared. The lights are dim. A follow spot fires into the boxes, audience looks up with a gathering commotion.

Angier is standing on the rail of the royal box, thirty feet above the stalls. He smiles down at the audience.

Man's reach exceeds his IMAGINATION!

The audience breaks into a massive standing ovation.

INT. BORDEN'S WORKSHOP – DAY

Fallon is at the workbench, staring at a sketch of Tesla's machine. Borden paces, agitated.

> BORDEN
> Why only a hundred performances? Do his methods dictate it, or is it simply a publicity move?

Borden walks back and stares at the sketch.

> Fifty yards in a second. And all I know is that he uses a trap-door. What's going on under that stage?

EXT. SCALA THEATRE – NIGHT

The theatre is closed, and three Blind Stagehands are wrestling a tarp-wrapped box onto a cart in the alleyway behind the theatre.

Fallon is watching from the shadows.

EXT. LABYRINTHINE STREETS – CONTINUOUS

Fallon shadows the cart as it slowly makes its way.

EXT. ABANDONED THEATRE – LATER

Fallon watches from further down the alley as the Blind Stagehands unload the box onto a dolly and wheel it through the stage door.

He moves closer, then stops. Seeing something. Cutter has emerged from a nearby doorway and slipped through the stage door.

INT. ABANDONED THEATRE – CONTINUOUS

The Blind Stagehands wheel the tarp-covered box to a large hole underneath the derelict stage and start hooking it up to a winch.

Cutter steps up onto the broken stage. Watching.

> BLIND STAGEHAND
>
> WHO'S THERE!

The man turns precisely to Cutter, flashing his white eyes.

> CUTTER
>
> It's Cutter.

> BLIND STAGEHAND
>
> What do you want?

> CUTTER
>
> I'm looking for Angier.

> ANGIER
> *(out of shot)*
>
> You found him.

Cutter turns. Angier approaches.

> I told you, John – I don't want you backstage on this one.

Cutter looks from Angier to the hole in the floor. Shrugs.

INT. BORDEN'S WORKSHOP – DAY

Borden sits at his workbench. Fallon fiddles with his bowler hat.

> BORDEN
>
> They do this every night. After each performance?

Fallon nods. Borden gets to his feet with a sigh. Turns to a poster on the wall –

THE GREAT DANTON PERFORMS
THE REAL TRANSPORTED MAN
100 SHOWS ONLY

He studies the image of Angier. There is a small devil looking over his shoulder.

> We're done. (*Turns to Fallon.*) Let him have his trick. You're not to go back there. I don't need to know his secret. Leave him alone.

Fallon puts on his hat with a shrug.

INT. SCALA THEATRE – EVENING

A packed house. Many hands raised. Move in on a Bearded Man, his gloved hand tentatively rising into the air. It is Borden.

A Glamorous Assistant beckons Borden from the aisle. He shuffles along his row towards her. Embarrassed.

Borden and four other Volunteers follow the Assistant down towards the stage . . .

On which stands Angier, leaning on his cane, smiling. Looming over him is the large and complex electrical machine. Borden stares at the machine as he mounts the stage.

Borden, fascinated, and the other Volunteers look over the vast machine, as Angier gestures theatrically at the various features of the metal and glass apparatus.

As the Assistant leads the Volunteers to the side of the stage, Borden slips through the gap at the side of the curtains –

INT. SCALA THEATRE, BACKSTAGE – CONTINUOUS

– looks around, disoriented, then darts for some stairs leading below stage where he runs into a burly Stagehand.

STAGEHAND
Where'd you think you're going?!

Borden pulls off his beard.

BORDEN

I'm part of the act, you fool!

The Stagehand raises his eyebrows and steps aside. Borden races down below the stage. Cutter approaches the Stagehand.

CUTTER

Who was that?

INT. SCALA THEATRE, ONSTAGE – CONTINUOUS

Angier throws switches on his machine. As it groans into life, sparking and crackling, Angier gazes at it, forgetting his audience. Entranced. Possessed.

INT. BENEATH THE STAGE – CONTINUOUS

Borden fumbles through the darkened area, lit by flashes and sparks through gaps in the boards of the stage above. He gasps as a flash illuminates a Stagehand with solid white eyes sitting nearby. Borden waves a hand in front of the Stagehand's face. He is blind. Borden moves on.

INT. SCALA THEATRE, ONSTAGE – NIGHT

Angier, facing the audience, steps backwards into the machine. He looks up at the electricity sparking just above him.

INT. BENEATH THE STAGE – CONTINUOUS

Borden lights a match. In front of him is a large glass tank filled with water, its lid propped open. Borden frowns.

INT. SCALA THEATRE, ONSTAGE – NIGHT

Bolts of electricity draw inwards, wrapping Angier in a ball of lightning which cracks.

INT. BENEATH THE STAGE – CONTINUOUS

The room fills with light as a trap-door snaps open and a body drops into the tank. The lid of the tank and trap-door above snap shut, leaving the tank, and Borden, in complete darkness.

INT. SCALA THEATRE, ONSTAGE – CONTINUOUS

The Machine sputters to a stop. Angier is gone. The audience sits, waiting.

INT. BENEATH THE STAGE – NIGHT

Borden lights another match. Stares in horror.

Inside the tank, Angier is drowning. His rolling eyes fixed on Borden, he pounds desperately on the thick glass, screaming bubbles . . .

Borden, horrified, tries forcing the lid of the tank open. It's sealed shut. He leaves the tank and begins searching around under the stage. He finds a spanner.

Borden smashes again and again at the glass of the tank, which spiders, then cracks, and finally gives way.

Water bursts from the tank, sweeping Angier's body into Borden, and both of them onto the ground.

Above them we can hear yelling. Borden rolls Angier onto his side and pounds on his back. Water and blood ooze from the man's lungs. His eyes are dilated and lifeless.

Angier is dead.

Borden is frozen, unable to move.

Cutter appears behind him, shocked by what he sees. Borden turns to look at him, his eyes wild with confusion.

                         CUTTER
          What did you do?

INT. MORGUE – DAY

A Mortician pulls back a sheet draped over a corpse.

Angier's lifeless eyes stare up at us. Cutter looks at Angier, then up at the Mortician. Nods.

                          JUDGE
                     (*voice-over*)
        Alfred Borden, you have been found guilty of the murder
        of Robert Angier . . .

INT. COURTROOM – DAY

Borden stands chained to the dock. The Judge has a piece of black cloth draped over his wig.

                          JUDGE
        You will, in one month's time, be hanged by the neck until
        dead. May the Lord have mercy on your soul.

INT. EVIDENCE ROOM, WAREHOUSE – DAY

A Policeman shows Owens into the room, walking him past all of the equipment to the far end, where Cutter stands staring at the machine's crate.

                          OWENS
        Mr Cutter?

Cutter turns.

        Owens.

They shake hands.

                          CUTTER
        Thank you for coming, Mr Owens. It's fallen to me to
        dispose of Mr Angier's equipment. Looking at the manifest,
        it's clear that Lord Caldlow has purchased the bulk of the
        items.

OWENS

Mr Cutter, if you needed to know where to deliver the
items you surely could have just –

CUTTER

It's not just that, Mr Owens. There is a particular item
(*Turns to crate.*) This item, in fact, that I wish to . . . well,
that is to say, I want to –

OWENS

You want to buy it instead.

CUTTER

I suppose so, yes.

Owens moves closer to the crate. Sees the COLORADO SPRINGS *stencil.*

OWENS

This is the machine? (*Off look.*) I'm afraid Lord Caldlow
was adamant about procuring this particular item.

CUTTER

Perhaps if I could talk to Lord Caldlow in person?

OWENS

Out of the question, I'm afraid.

Cutter nods. Owens starts to walk away. Turns.

Of course, I suppose . . . if, in the course of your delivery
arrangements your paths were to cross . . . I can't stop you
from speaking your mind.

Cutter nods.

INT. CELL, NEWGATE PRISON – MORNING

Borden sits quietly. Sullen opens the door.

SULLEN
(*sardonic*)

Still here, Borden?

Borden looks up.

BORDEN

For now.

SULLEN

Got a visitor. Lord Caldlow. With a little girl.

Borden hurries to his feet.

EXT. PRISON YARD, NEWGATE PRISON – DAY

Borden, clutching an envelope, is escorted around the courtyard walkway, peering at the stairs. He catches a glimpse of his daughter walking beside a man. His eyes light up and he hurries to the fence.

As Borden reaches the fence he crouches to greet his little girl.

BORDEN

Jess, how are you?

Jess smiles at him and reaches through the fence.

Are you alright?

She nods.

I've missed you. Fallon's missed you. We both have.

Borden drinks in her face, her hair. She grasps the fence.

JESS

Can I come in there, Daddy?

BORDEN

Everything's going to be okay.

It is only then that he notices the hand on her shoulder. He rises to come face to face with Lord Caldlow –

You must be Lord –

– who is Robert Angier. Risen from the dead.

ANGIER
(*English accent*)

Caldlow. Yes, I am. I always have been.

Borden stares at Angier.

133

BORDEN

I saw you die.

Angier just smiles.

ANGIER

They flatter you with all those chains, Alfred. Don't they know you can't escape without your little rubber ball?

Borden says nothing.

All I wanted to do was prove that I was the better magician. But you couldn't leave me alone.

BORDEN

You were always afraid to get your hands dirty . . . (*Looks down at Jess.*) Not any more.

ANGIER

No. Not any more. And I win. Because no one cares about the man in the box, the man who disappears.

BORDEN

You win. But don't take my little girl . . .

Angier looks at Borden. Bitter.

ANGIER

I *know* how hard it is to have someone so precious taken away, don't I, Borden? But you can't take her with you now, can you? She'll be looked after. Goodbye, Professor.

Angier gently pulls Jess back from the fence. She protests. Desperate, Borden holds out the envelope.

BORDEN

Wait. Don't you want this? You paid for it.

ANGIER

Your secret?

Borden nods. Angier steps up, takes the envelope.

You always were the better magician, Borden. We both know that.

He tears the envelope in half. Then again. And again . . .

But whatever your secret was, you'll have to agree –

He tosses the pieces into the courtyard below.

(*Victorious.*) – mine is better.

Angier turns.

> BORDEN
> Angier! Let me say goodbye. Please.

Angier stops. Lets Jess come to fence. She is crying.

> JESS
> When are you taking me home, Daddy?

> BORDEN
> Soon. I promise. Soon.

> ANGIER
> For God's sake, Borden.

> BORDEN
> Daddy's coming, I promise. I promise. Here –

Borden produces his rubber ball. Jess looks at it.

I promise.

Borden vanishes the rubber ball. Angier pulls Jess back from the fence and starts walking away. Borden rises.

You think this place can hold me, Angier?!

Angier continues walking Jess away. Shaking his head.

Angier!

EXT. LARGE COUNTRY ESTATE – DAY

Angier steps out of an ornate carriage with Jess.

INT. LARGE COUNTRY ESTATE – DAY

Angier steps inside with Jess. The Housekeeper comes to take her.

HOUSEKEEPER

Come here, love. (*To Angier.*) Sir, there's a gentleman waiting.

Angier looks at her, surprised.

INT. DRAWING ROOM, COUNTRY ESTATE – DAY – CONTINUOUS

Cutter is in the drawing room, looking at the carriage clock on the mantel. Angier enters. Cutter spots his reflection.

CUTTER

Dear God.

ANGIER

Hello, Cutter.

CUTTER

You're alive.

Angier nods.

You're Lord Caldlow.

Angier nods again.

How?

ANGIER
(*shrugs*)

I learned an American accent from –

CUTTER
(*angry*)

How are you alive, Robert?! I saw you on the slab, for God's sake.

Angier fixes Cutter with a steady gaze.

ANGIER

A magician never reveals his secrets.

The Housekeeper appears with Jess at her side.

HOUSEKEEPER

Go on, child.

Goodnight, sir.

Angier smiles kindly at her.

ANGIER

Goodnight, Jess.

They leave.

CUTTER

Who's the girl?

Angier says nothing.

I've seen her. I've seen her in court with Fallon . . .

Cutter, realising, looks at Angier, shocked.

(*Quiet.*) What have you done?

ANGIER

She needs looking after –

CUTTER

She needs her father, but you're letting him hang. And
I helped you.

Cutter moves to the door. In a daze. Pauses.

I came here tonight to beg Lord Caldlow to let me destroy
that machine. But I won't beg you for anything.

ANGIER

You don't have to. I'm going to make sure the machine is
never used again. (*Shrugs.*) A good magician never repeats
his tricks.

Cutter considers this. Makes a decision.

CUTTER

Then, Lord Caldlow, where would you like me to deliver it?

ANGIER

My theatre. It belongs with the Prestige materials.

EXT. PRISON YARD, NEWGATE PRISON – MORNING

Borden is at the fence. Fallon is on the other side.

BORDEN

We go alone now – both of us. Only I don't have as far to go as you.

Borden looks down at his feet.

You were right. I should've left him to his damned trick . . . I'm sorry. I'm sorry for so many things. For Sarah. I didn't want to hurt her.

Fallon wipes tears from his face. Borden looks at him.

Don't cry. Not for me. Go live your life in full. For both of us.

Borden pulls the rubber ball from his pocket and bounces it up and down. He turns to be led back into the prison, dropping the ball.

The ball bounces gently past the fence. Fallon catches it.

EXT. PRISON CORRIDOR, NEWGATE PRISON – NIGHT

Borden is led along the walkway, braced by six Guards. And a Priest.

The procession stops at the gate at the bottom of the stairs. Sullen opens the gate and Borden is led through. As Borden passes Sullen, he leans in to his ear.

BORDEN
(*quiet*)

Are you watching closely?

Sullen stares back at him, terrified.

EXT. GALLOWS, NEWGATE PRISON – CONTINUOUS

The room is low and small. Two parallel beams, eight feet high, run from one wall to the other. Hanging from the centre of the beams is a chain. Below the chain is a trap-door.

Sullen locks the door to the chamber.

EXT. LARGE COUNTRY ESTATE – DAY

Jess is playing in the grounds. A Nursemaid some distance off chats to a Gardener.

Jess looks up from playing. Someone is there. Cutter.

EXT. ABANDONED THEATRE – EVENING

A cart pulls up to the side of the theatre.

Cutter and two Workmen step down from the cart and move to the back of it. Cutter pulls the tarp off the back of the cart. Underneath it is the machine's crate.

INT. ABANDONED THEATRE – EVENING

The crate is sitting on the dolly in the auditorium.

> CUTTER
> Thank you, gents.

> WORKMAN
> Where do you want it?

> CUTTER
> Don't worry. Someone's coming to help.

The Workmen leave. Cutter looks at the crate.

Angier emerges from the darkness.

EXT. GALLOWS – NIGHT

The Warders remove Borden's chains and shackles and replace them with strong leather belts that bind his feet together and his hands to his sides.

They shuffle him forward onto the trap-door.

INT. ABANDONED THEATRE – NIGHT

Angier and Cutter load the crate onto a platform suspended by a rope and position it over the hole.

Cutter begins turning a winch, lowering the crate. Angier indicates a pile of bricks and a bag of sand.

                    CUTTER
    I'm bricking this over after we're done.

                    ANGIER
    Cautious as ever, Cutter. No one's going to use the place.
    I own it.

INT. CELLAR, ABANDONED THEATRE — EVENING

Angier slowly climbs down a ladder from the hole to join Cutter in the darkness below.

Cutter is standing next to the platform and the crate. The only light comes from a lantern Angier is carrying. We can see only a small flicker of the high mouldy walls of the cellar, but it is a large open space.

                    CUTTER
    No room left – you couldn't have accommodated a
    hundred performances.

                    ANGIER
    A good thing I retired early, then.

Angier puts the lantern and his cane on the lid of the crate and the two men heft it off the platform.

    We'll put it down the end.

Angier and Cutter move into the darkness with the crate. From the small pool of light afforded by the lantern, we can see that they are navigating their way through a large space filled with large glass boxes.

They arrive at the end and set the crate down.

                    CUTTER
    I'll go mix the cement.

Cutter looks at Angier, cold.

    Take a minute to consider your achievement.

Cutter turns.

                    ANGIER
    Cutter, I tried not to involve you.

Cutter looks back at Angier. Sad.

                    CUTTER
    I once told you about the sailor who described drowning
    to me . . .

                    ANGIER
                    (*nods*)
    He said it was like going home.

                    CUTTER
    I was lying. He said it was agony.

Cutter looks at Angier. Then disappears into darkness.

INT. ABANDONED THEATRE – MOMENTS LATER

Cutter comes across the stage and up through the auditorium.

Fallon is coming in the other direction.

As they pass they nod gravely at each other.

EXT. GALLOWS, NEWGATE PRISON – NIGHT

*Borden is held in place on the trap-door by two Warders. The
Hangman walks up behind him and attaches a noose to the chain
hanging above Borden. He slips the other end of the noose over
Borden's neck. Positions it under Borden's jaw.*

INT. CELLAR, ABANDONED THEATRE – CONTINUOUS

*Angier is alone, bathed in the light of the lantern. He turns to the
nearest glass box and smooths a hand along its face.*

                    ANGIER
                    (*whisper*)
    No one cares about the man in the box.

Behind him, a noise.

>   (*Calling.*) Cutter?

No response.

EXT. GALLOWS, NEWGATE PRISON – NIGHT

The Warden looks at Borden.

>   WARDEN
> Alfred Borden, on this day, in the name of the King and the
> High Court of England, you will meet your end. Do you
> have anything to say for yourself?

*Borden says nothing. The Warden gestures to the Hangman, who
begins to pull the lever.*

>   BORDEN
>   (*whisper*)
>   Abracadabra.

*The trap drops from under Borden and he falls into the room below.
His rope snaps to a halt.*

INT. CELLAR, ABANDONED THEATRE – NIGHT

Angier peers down the row of glass boxes with the lantern.

>   ANGIER
>   (*tense*)
>   CUTTER?

*Angier freezes. He can hear a small thud, thud, thud getting closer,
approaching from the darkness . . .*

Angier flinches as a rubber ball bounces into the light.

*Angier drops his cane to catch the ball. He turns it around in his
hands, confused.*

Light explodes around him as a gunshot rings out.

*Angier stands for a moment, confused, staring at the ball, then
collapses to the ground, clutching at his stomach.*

Fallon's bowler hat breaks into the circle of light. He is holding a smoking pistol . . .

Angier drops the ball and it rolls across the floor, coming to rest at Fallon's feet. But it is not Fallon's gloved hand that picks up the ball – it is a mutilated hand, with two and a half fingers missing. Angier looks up.

Alfred Borden removes the bowler hat and takes a bow.

> ANGIER
> (*weak*)

You – you died.

Borden shakes his head.

Realisation sweeps over Angier like a nightmare.

A brother. A twin.

INT. BASEMENT – CONTINUOUS – FLASHBACK

Fallon drops into the coffin. As Fallon stares up at us, we see, for the first time, something familiar in his face – Fallon is really Borden in disguise.

> ANGIER
> (*voice-over*)

You were Fallon. The whole time . . .

Fallon/Borden's face disappears as Cutter seals the coffin.

INT. CELLAR, ABANDONED THEATRE

Borden smiles.

> BORDEN

We were both Fallon. And we were both Borden.

Angier considers this. Mind spinning.

> ANGIER

Were you the one who went into the box –

INT. STAGE — EVENING — FLASHBACK

As the ball bounces across the stage, Borden steps into the cabinet, shutting the door behind him.

> ANGIER
> (*voice-over*)
> – or the one who came back out?

Borden steps out of the second cabinet and catches the ball.

INT. DRESSING ROOM — EVENING — FLASHBACK

A Stagehand wheels the two stage cabinets into the dressing room and leaves. Borden bolts the door after him.

> BORDEN
> (*voice-over*)
> We took turns. The trick is where we would swap . . .

Borden opens the first cabinet and pulls up the false bottom.

His twin brother, in identical stage clothes, uncurls himself from the hidden compartment and hauls himself out.

INT. WORKSHOP — LATER — FLASHBACK

Fallon and Borden are seated at the make-up table. Fallon begins removing pieces of his costume and make-up and handing them to the other brother. As we watch, they switch identities.

INT. CELLAR, ABANDONED THEATRE — EVENING

Angier stares up at Borden. Appalled.

> ANGIER
> Cutter knew. But I told him it was too simple. Too easy.

> BORDEN
> Simple, maybe. But not easy.

INT. WORKSHOP – EVENING – FLASHBACK

Both Bordens are standing at the workbench. One brother is gripping the other by his wrist and placing a chisel on his finger.

He checks the placement of the chisel against his own mutilated fingers, adjusts the chisel's position, then picks up the hammer.

> BORDEN
> (*voice-over*)
> Nothing easy about two men sharing one life.

The second brother swigs from a gin bottle, then bites down on a padded stick as the first brother brings down the hammer.

INT. CELLAR, ABANDONED THEATRE – EVENING

Borden stares at his mutilated hand clasping the rubber ball.

> ANGIER
> What about Olivia? And your wife?

> BORDEN
> We each loved one of them. We each had half a full life.
> Enough for us, but not for them.

Borden puts the ball in his pocket. Tears in his eyes.

> Sacrifice, Robert – that's the price of a good trick.

Borden looks down at Angier with contempt.

> But you wouldn't know anything about that, would you?

Angier is dying. He opens his mouth to talk, but his voice is so weak that Borden has to stoop to hear him.

> ANGIER
> (*very quiet*)
> I've made sacrifices.

> BORDEN
> It takes nothing to steal someone else's work.

> ANGIER
> It takes everything.

INT. ABANDONED THEATRE – DAY – FLASHBACK

Angier stands in front of Tesla's machine. Loading the pistol. He places the pistol by the machine . . .

Angier takes off his jacket and steps towards the hissing machine. Bolts curl themselves around him.

Angier hurls himself into the light.

This time we do not cut away.

The machine sputters out.

Angier is still standing beneath it.

> ANGIER
> (*confused*)
> It didn't work.

> VOICE
> (*out of shot*)
> Yes it did.

Angier turns . . .

Another Angier is standing on the chalk hash-mark, steam rising off his shoulders.

The first Angier lunges for the pistol and levels it at the second Angier.

> SECOND ANGIER
> (*horrified*)
> No, wait! I'm the –

Bang! Bang! The first Angier fires two shots and, grim-faced, drops the pistol. Shocked, he stumbles back, in a daze, clothes still steaming.

INT. CELLAR, ABANDONED THEATRE – NIGHT

Angier looks down, a slight smile on his face. He gestures to the lantern.

> ANGIER
> (*weaker*)
> Do you want to see what it cost me? You didn't see where you are, did you? Let me show you.

Angier slumps to the floor as he tries to reach for the lantern. He can't get his hand to obey him.

It took courage to climb into that machine every night . . .

INT. UNDER THE STAGE – EVENING – FLASHBACK

A drowning tank, identical to the one we have already seen. A Blind Stagehand sits behind it, smoking.

                              ANGIER
                            (*voice-over*)
          Not knowing if I'd be the Prestige . . .

Suddenly, a trap-door flashes open as Angier falls from the stage above and splashes into the tank. The lid snaps shut.

Or the man in the box . . .

Angier pounds on the glass, frantic. The Blind Stagehand continues smoking. Oblivious.

INT. WORKSHOP – DAY – FLASHBACK

Two hands slam shut on the lid of a birdcage.

EXT. SCALA THEATRE – EVENING – FLASHBACK

The Blind Stagehands are wrestling a large crate onto a cart in the alleyway behind the theatre.

INT. CELLAR, ABANDONED THEATRE – NIGHT

Angier stops trying to move and leans back, resigned.

                              BORDEN
                             (*scorn*)
          You went halfway around the world. You spent a fortune.
          You did terrible things . . . and all of it for nothing.

Angier looks up at him with his last spark of competitiveness.

ANGIER

Nothing? You never understood, did you? Why we did this?
(*Coughs.*) The audience knows the truth – that the world is
simple. Miserable. Solid all the way through. But if you
could fool them, even for a second, you could make them
wonder. Then you got to see something very special . . .
(*Coughs, looks up.*) You really don't know?

Borden just stares at Angier. Who smiles.

It was the look on their faces.

*Angier's body topples over, knocking over the lantern. Borden steps
back as the oil spreads, flaming, from the lantern.*

CUTTER
(*voice-over*)
Every magic trick consists of three parts, or acts . . .

Borden watches Angier for a moment, then turns to leave.

INT. WORKSHOP – DAY

*The workshop from the opening of the film. We now recognise it as
Borden's. Cutter performs the birdcage trick for the Little Girl we now
know as Jess.*

CUTTER
(*voice-over*)
The first part is called the Pledge.

Cutter is showing her the canary.

INT. ABANDONED THEATRE – NIGHT

The burning lamp oil spreads light through the cellar . . .

CUTTER
(*voice-over*)
The second part is called the Turn. I take the ordinary
something . . .

Angier lies in his pooling blood.

And I make it do something extraordinary . . .

Angier's eyes move around, looking at the shapes around him increasingly illuminated by the hellish light . . .

INT. WORKSHOP – DAY

Cutter whips the shawl away – cage and bird have disappeared.

> CUTTER
> (*voice-over*)
>
> But you wouldn't clap yet.

Jess stares, expectant. Cutter holds up his handkerchief-covered hand.

> Because making something disappear isn't enough . . .

Cutter whips the handkerchief from his hand, revealing a canary. Just then, Jess sees something and jumps off the chest, running past him . . .

> You have to bring it back.

Borden is in the doorway – Jess leaps into his arms. Borden holds her tight. Looks at Cutter, who is putting on his coat. Nods. Cutter leaves.

Borden reaches into his pocket and hands Jess his rubber ball. She smiles, then buries her head in his neck.

INT. ABANDONED THEATRE – NIGHT

Borden stops at the ladder. He notices the shadows from the burning oil playing on the walls . . .

> CUTTER
> (*voice-over*)
>
> Now you're looking for the secret . . .

Borden turns slowly to look back into the cellar, peering into the flickering light of the burning lamp oil.

> But you won't find it . . .

Borden stares back into the cellar. What he sees puts a look on his face that is beyond words.

Large glass tanks. Dozens of them. Row after row stretching into the cavernous cellar.

 . . . because you don't *really* want to know . . .

Floating in each and every tank, dressed in rotting stage clothes, is yet another Robert Angier.

INT. ABANDONED THEATRE – DAY

Cutter spreads mortar on the last brick of the wall he has built in the opening to the cellar.

He places the brick in the wall, sealing it up.

EXT. FOREST – DAY – FLASHBACK

A cat slinks its way through a pile of top hats, knocking one over as it disappears into the forest beyond.

> CUTTER
> (*voice-over*)
 . . . you want to be fooled.

We are left alone in the glade, staring at the top hats.

Fade out.

Credits.

End.